THE CRUCIBLE OF MODERN THOUGHT

THE CRUCIBLE OF MODERN THOUGHT

WHAT IS GOING INTO IT;
WHAT IS HAPPENING THERE;
WHAT IS TO COME OUT OF IT?

A STUDY OF THE PREVAILING MENTAL UNREST

BY

WILLIAM WALKER ATKINSON

GYAN

Published by

Gyan Publishing House
5, Ansari Road
Daryaganj, New Delhi-110002
Phone: 011-47034999, 9811692060
E-mail: books@gyanbooks.com

Distribution Network
gyanbooks.com
India, USA, Canada, UK, Australia

ISBN: 978-93-6208-107-0 (PB)
First Published, 1910

2nd Impression 2024

Printed at: Gyan Press, Delhi.

THE CRUCIBLE OF MODERN THOUGHT
Author: WILLIAM WALKER ATKINSON

THE CRUCIBLE OF MODERN THOUGHT

THE CRUCIBLE OF MODERN THOUGHT

WHAT IS GOING INTO IT;
WHAT IS HAPPENING THERE;
WHAT IS TO COME OUT OF IT?

A STUDY OF THE PREVAILING MENTAL UNREST

BY

WILLIAM WALKER ATKINSON

"And the word of the Lord came unto me . . . . Saying, What seest thou? And I said, I see a seething pot."

Jeremiah I:13.

L. N. FOWLER & CO.
7 Imperial Arcade, Ludgate Circus
LONDON, E. C.

1910
THE PROGRESS COMPANY
CHICAGO.

CONTENTS

CONTENTS

PREFACE

This book is an outgrowth of a series of articles originally published in *The Progress Magazine* under a pseudonym, in which I sought to account for the prevailing mental unrest regarding subjects of religious and philosophical import. These articles attracted much attention from careful students of the times, and there have been many requests for the republication thereof in book form under my own name. Accordingly, the publishers of the articles requested me to revise the several papers, and to add thereto such further matter as I might think proper. I have gone over the original articles, taking away a little here and adding much there. Several entirely new subjects have been considered and inserted in their proper places in the text. At least one-third of the present book is entirely new, having been added to the revised form of the original articles. I have purposely quoted freely from good authorities, that the reader may have the benefit of the thought of a number of competent persons upon the various phases of the subject, in addition to what I have personally thought and written. I have sought merely to tell my story in a plain, simple manner, without any attempt at fine writing, literary excellence, or display of technical philosophical knowledge. My desire has been to place in the hands of the everyday busy man and woman a book from the pages of which they may gain a general knowledge of the causes of the modern mental unrest—an idea of what is going into this great melting pot of thought; what is happening there; and what is likely to be poured forth from it. To many, the numerous new "isms," "ologies" and cults, are entirely new—something sprung full-grown from the brains of their founders. The absence of an elementary acquaintance with the history of philosophy, on the part of the average man and woman, has given to many new prophets and founders of cults an unmerited and unwarranted importance and authority. I trust that this book will enable some of those who have been perplexed and worried over these new (?) "isms," and teachings, to learn the true sources of those startling conglomerations of metaphysics, philosophy and theology, and thus once more to regain their mental bearings. It is also my hope that some who have a tendency toward philosophical study may be inspired by this book to go to the proper sources of such knowledge—to the masters of this branch of thought—instead of sitting at the feet of the, too often, freakish, irresponsible, and *bizarre* founders and teachers of the pseudo-schools and cults, who have been revamping the old teachings, dressing them in fantastic garb, and offering them (usually at a high rate of compensation) to those who have felt the hunger for wisdom and the thirst for information, but who lacked the knowledge of the places where these things could be had at first hand, pure and free from the adulterations of these self-constituted middle-men in the great market of Philosophy.

WILLIAM WALKER ATKINSON.

Chicago, Ill., Oct. 18, 1910.

The Crucible of Modern Thought

CHAPTER I

THE TWENTIETH CENTURY MELTING POT

Everyone who has kept in touch with the current of the modern trend of thought must be aware of the operation of the mighty processes of tearing down, building up, rearrangement and reconstruction now under way in the realm of thought—in every region of that realm, in fact. It may be well said that modern thought is in the melting pot, and that even the most careful observers are in ignorance of what will finally come from that pot. Advanced thinkers along all lines of human knowledge have tossed their conceptions into the great crucible of Twentieth Century Thought, there to mingle with the conceptions of others and to be fused into some wonderful new combination, the exact nature of which is beyond the knowing of even the most prescient thinker among us. Of course, each contributor, or class of contributors, to the mass of material which is placed into the great melting pot, feels assured that his or her particular material must necessarily be the predominant element in the new composition—that their particular theory will be in strong evidence in the new synthesis.

But the thinker who stands aloof, who assumes the judicial frame of mind, who regards the process from the viewpoint affording the proper perspective, does not feel at all sure of the final outcome. He sees the general trend of the thought currents, but he also recognizes the operation of reaction following action, of the play of the opposite poles of thought—and he reserves his final judgment of the outcome—and waits, and waits. The answer lies in the future—the present is merely the scene of the struggle and bubble. The materials of the new composition are being tossed into the great pot, one by one, each day adding new materials which will operate in determining the nature of the composite substance which will be poured forth in the end, and which will then go through the slow process of cooling and crystallization. But he is either a thoughtless man, a bold man, or an inspired prophet, who dares venture to predict the exact nature of that which will come out of the crucible when all this heterogeneous mass of crude material shall have been melted, fused and amalgamated.

One seeking for the causes of this modern unrest in the world of thought must go far back in the pages of philosophy in his search. For much of the modern activity arises from causes latent in the thought of hundreds, yes, thousands, of years ago. There has been a constant evolution of thought, with its action and reaction, its manifestation of the opposing poles of activity, its tides and currents, its slipping back and its recovery of lost ground. In this evolution there has been noticed the constant swing of the pendulum of thought from one extreme to another, and then back again—the curious manifestation of fashion in thought which causes a favorite set of ideas to flourish for a while and then to sink into obscurity, there to remain for centuries, only to spring up again with renewed vigor after the passage of years. Strange as it may appear to many, nearly all of the great modern philosophical truths have been known in the past and have gone through this period of obscurement and hiding, only to now emerge on the scene of modern thought in full vigor, claiming their rightful place in the evolution of thought.

It must be admitted, however, that the modern scientific spirit—that spirit which seeks truth for truth's sake—which follows reason wherever it may lead, irrespective of the personal beliefs, theories and opinions of the investigators—seems to be unique and peculiar to this age. Never before in the history of human thought has there been manifested such an honest desire for the real truth as at present. We see thinkers and investigators sorrowfully, but willingly, discarding many of their old and hallowed ideas and beliefs, because investigation has shown the unreasonableness of such beliefs. The spirit of the materialists, who, in their search for evidence that matter was the final and ultimate reality, found instead that matter, in the old sense, melted into mystery and became non-existent, and who then gladly accepted the new knowledge, is but one evidence of the modern scientific spirit which is animating the world's best thinkers. The courage and honesty of many of the thinkers along theological lines, who find it necessary to throw overboard their old dogmas, as the price of the discovery of higher conceptions of truth, is akin to the instance just cited, and requires even greater courage and honesty of purpose.

While this unrest in the world of thought seems to be scattered over a large and varied field, yet if we will but closely examine into the underlying causes, we will see that all these varied manifestations and phases of the unrest really arise from the changing foundations of popular philosophy. And, indeed, the basic thought upon which philosophy rests is involved in the shifting and readjustment. That basic thought is that which men call the idea of fundamental principles, and which underlies all philosophic thought, as the foundation-stones underlie every edifice. A shifting of that foundation brings down the house, or at least disturbs its equilibrium, cracks its walls, and necessitates radical and important repairs. And this is what has happened in the world of thought to-day. The ideas regarding fundamental principles are changing, and the structure of thought erected thereupon is endangered—its walls are cracking, its beams slipping, its floors sagging, its roof is awry. Just how great the damage—just the extent of the repairs needed—these can be determined only by time, for the shifting and slipping of the foundation is still under way. Some think it will be necessary to tear down the walls and erect an entirely new edifice upon the readjusted foundation—who knows?

This claim that the conception of the fundamental principles is being disturbed, and is thus causing the trouble in the edifice of modern thought, may seem strange to those who have thought that the discoveries in physical science and the unrest in sociological thought were the disturbing elements. But the careful thinker will see that the real disturbance lies far deeper than these. For these conceptions depend materially, at least in their application and working-out, upon the world's conception of the fundamental principles supporting the phenomenal universe. All edifices of thought must be built upon some foundation, and the only true foundation for thought is the conception of the fundamental principles, upon which depend the particular conception of philosophy, nature and life built thereupon. At the last, all physical conceptions must rest upon the basis of some metaphysical conception. This may not be apparent at first thought, but a retracing of the steps of reasoning will show that the statement is correct. The parable of the house that is built upon shifting sand, and that built upon the solid rock, is in accordance with the facts of thought and philosophy. It sometimes happens, however, that what has been thought to be a foundation of solid rock is finally discovered to be but soft crumbling sandstone, which is rapidly disintegrating into shifting sand. And this is what appears to be the trouble to-day. The foundation is apparently crumbling, or at least settling in a new adjustment of itself. And the settling or crumbling process is disturbing thought and life in all of its many phases.

Let us now examine the case of this shifting or crumbling foundation. Let us see, if possible, the nature and extent of the damage. In order to proceed intelligently we must, for the time being, discard our prejudices and maintain the open mind. Let us examine what men are saying and thinking about the matter, and then proceed to make up our minds regarding the true state of affairs. This is the purpose of this book, and this only. I shall not try to convert anyone to my own particular views on the subject. In fact, I shall endeavor to keep my own views in the background. Instead of appearing as the counsel for the prosecution or the defense, I shall try to occupy the seat of the judge—instead of making the argument of counsel on either side, I shall try to follow the course of the judge in summing up and reviewing the evidence and submitting the same to the jury of the readers of this book. This is the only fair way, and I trust that you, the jury, will give me the credit for fairness and just intentions as we proceed.

The idea of fundamental principles depends upon the conception of an underlying something, in which philosophy holds that everything that is must "live and move and have its being." The human mind has ever tended toward the conception of a Something underlying all individual manifestations of being—the ocean of being, in which all particular beings are but as drops or particles. This universal principle of being has been variously conceived of as being by nature anything or everything from pure spirit to pure matter. Theologians have conceived of it as a mysterious something called spirit, connected in some way with Deity. Philosophers have endeavored to attribute to it various and different natures. Modern science has considered it either as the principle of matter, on the one hand, or as "that infinite and eternal energy from which all things proceed," as Spencer put it, on the other hand. Ancient Oriental metaphysicians, as well as modern idealism, have considered it as pure mind. Ancient pantheism and modern transcendentalism have regarded Being as identical with Deity. Between these various conceptions the metaphysical and philosophical conflict has raged.

While, at first, it may seem that the conflict is one which concerns only theologians, philosophers and metaphysicians, a closer examination will reveal the fact that its influence and scope extends much farther, inasmuch as our conceptions of life, action, duty, morals and general conduct must, and do, depend materially upon the conception of Being held by the popular mind. The individual may be uncertain or indifferent, but, nevertheless, he is affected and, to a certain extent, bound by the ideas arising from such popular conception. The affairs of men's lives depend upon certain standards, and these standards depend upon the popular conception regarding the source of standards, and the belief in and acceptance of the authority of the standard-makers. These standards may be said to have the effect of laws, and the efficacy of all laws must rest upon the acceptance by the people of the authority, reality and power of the lawmaker to enforce. Therefore, any disturbance regarding the validity of the standards and values of life must arise from a shifting conception regarding the fundamental source of these standards, values and laws, in the public mind. And this is what we mean when we say that the foundation of the structure of thought and action gives signs of a shifting, settling, or sinking. This foundation is, of course, in the public mind, and we must look to the public mind for the evidences of the changes that are going on.

Remember, first and last, that I am not attempting to pass upon the truth or untruth of any particular conceptions of the fundamental truths—neither am I undertaking to theorize or speculate upon the real nature of truth. We are merely conducting an investigation into the state of the public mind on the subject—merely feeling the pulse of modern thought. Upon the fundamental conceptions in the public mind depend the actions and life of the individuals composing that public. Not only is it true that a tree is known by its fruits, but it is also true that *the fruits may be known by its tree.* We may infer the popular standards by observing the actions of the populace; we may predicate the actions of the populace by knowing the public standards. And the standards must, in the end, depend upon the accepted idea or conception of the fundamental principles. Investigate the subject from any starting point, and we find ourselves approaching the center at last.

In considering the conception of the fundamental principles and its effect on the creation of standards of living and action, we need go back no further than the Middle Ages. That particular period of the history of the race shows in itself a reactionary swing of the pendulum of thought. Independent thought had reached its lowest ebb. Here and there were to be found a thinker or two who dared use his reason, but the philosophies of the past were forgotten or unknown to the masses of people, and dogmatic theology had spread its wet blanket over the embers of independent thought so thoroughly as to almost smother out of existence even its feeble spark.

There was no question regarding fundamental principles disturbing the public mind of the Middle Ages. Everything of the kind had been positively and thoroughly settled by the church. The world had been created out of nothing, in six days, some 5,000 years before that time; the animals had been made, one by one, species by species, and man was a special creation, coming after all the earth had been prepared for him. He had partaken of the forbidden fruit and had been driven from Eden, and the curse of original sin had been placed on the race. There were no disputed questions of geology, anthropology or general science. The earth was flat, and the sun and stars moved around it—this relieved the minds of the people of all worrisome questions of astronomy—the nebular hypothesis was undreamed of. Ethics and morality were likewise beyond dispute or argument—these matters had been settled once and for all by the scriptures interpreted by the infallible authority of the church. Theologians disputed about doctrinal points—but this did not concern the general public, for the latter knew nothing of these subjects. The authority was supreme—the standards were firmly established—there was nothing to think about. Some failed to live up to the standards, but the standards were fixed, nevertheless.

Time rolled on. Printing was discovered, and people began to read books. Then came the theological revolts which resulted in the establishment of various churches in opposition to the one church. People began to realize that it was possible and permissible to reason about things instead of having to accept them upon mere authority. The Reformation, as it is called, was the entering wedge of independent thought. People actually dared to question the authority of the church, and, wonder upon wonders, they were not struck dead on the spot! The chains were loosened and the primal causes of the present unrest were set into motion. As time passed the churches disputed one with another, and various sects and divisions arose, each of which based its schism upon some disputed conception of doctrine or practice. After a time the members of the various sects began to hold individual opinions, although still adhering to general truths and creeds. Creeds became broader, and men claimed a greater and still greater right of individual interpretation and freer thought. Although the educated classes did the most of the thinking, still, as is always the case, their opinions gradually filtered through to the lower classes and changes became general.

During the eighteenth century there was a great activity in Europe along the lines of freethought.

All sorts of heretical schools became popular—from atheism to modified deism. People also began to rebel against the constituted authorities—the doctrine of divine right began to be doubted. The French Revolution was an active factor in the shaking off of old ideals, political and theological, and although a reaction set in following the terrible excess of fanatics of the times, still the work had been done, and much of the leaven remained. The American Revolution, with its democratic teachings, and the heterodox views of men like Jefferson and Paine, added to the work done by the earlier leaders of the French Revolution, and the teachings of Voltaire and others of his school.

During the nineteenth century the advances of physical science made still further inroads into the orthodox teachings of the past. Reaching the half-way point of the century, men like Darwin, Huxley, Tyndall and Herbert Spencer began to exert a remarkable influence upon the popular mind, and orthodoxy was put squarely on the defensive in a manner never before known—a condition which has continued even unto this day, the orthodox ranks having been steadily forced to retreat, until now many of the orthodox opinions are almost as heterodox as those of the skeptics of fifty or a hundred years ago. Many of the orthodox pulpits to-day give utterance to views almost identical with those which shocked our great-grandfathers when uttered by Thomas

Paine. The higher criticism of to-day goes further than the infidelism of 1850.

The theory of Evolution and the Descent of Man broke down many of the old barriers, and the works of Huxley and Spencer tore down still more. It became popular to be an evolutionist, and the adherents of the older teachings were regarded as behind the times. A strong tendency toward materialism set in, which many supposed was destined to sweep before it all the old line of defences of orthodoxy. But, strange to say, toward the close of the century a reaction set in. Although people had been carried away with the newer teachings which had wiped away old lines of thought, the old religious instinct and the desire for spiritual things had not been destroyed. All the stronger for having been suppressed for a time, these factors in the human mind swung back the pendulum of thought away from materialism. Materialism, once so popular in scientific circles and in the universities, has now almost entirely disappeared, being superseded by a new conception of idealism. There is, of course, an old guard of materialism still left, but its popularity has departed for the time being. But the pendulum, in its backward swing, did not carry popular thought back to the old orthodox standards. These had been discarded once and for all, it seemed. There was a need for a new set of conceptions—and the demand created the supply. And here we have the key to the present conditions of affairs.

Filling the vacuum created by the evaporation of the older orthodox dogmas, we find the ideals of ancient Greek philosophy, mingling with the still older teachings of the Hindus, and through all is heard the note of mysticism which has ever pervaded human thought in every religion, every time, and every race. The discarded and long-reviled teachings of the Gnostics, that body of early Christian mystics, have arisen again and under new names have found popular favor in the minds of the public of the twentieth century. The teachings of the old Hindu Vedantism, given a new impetus by Emerson and the transcendentalists, find a prominent place in the advancing thought of to-day. Plato has sprung into renewed and startling popular favor, and many advanced modern thinkers find in his pages the truths for which they have sought in vain elsewhere. Heraclitus finds corroboration in the teachings of modern science, and his views of the eternal change and the "becoming" of the universe are repeated in many modern teachings. Other bits of philosophy have been borrowed from Buddhism, and even from the Sufis, the mystic sect of Mohammedism. Even the philosophy of Lao-tze, the ancient Chinese philosopher who taught of the Tao, or "Way," is accepted as correctly representing some stages of modern thought. The new bottles of the present are being filled with the old wine of the past.

CHAPTER II

OLD WINE IN NEW BOTTLES

The thought of the twentieth century has drawn boldly upon the past centuries for its stores of wisdom and philosophy, and has appropriated the same boldly, and often without giving due credit. New sects, schools and cults have arisen, all exerting a certain influence upon the general thought of the day. Theosophy has acted as a leaven in the direction of popularizing the Hindu conceptions, particularly in the matter of the doctrine of reincarnation and rebirth. Christian Science has exerted an influence in the direction of idealism, recalling in some respects (independent of its features of healing) the idealistic teachings of the Vedanta and of the Grecian philosophers. Unitarianism has exerted a powerful influence among the churches, and its effects are seen even in the pulpits which revile it. The higher criticism in the churches, has tended to lead the public away from the old ideas to which they once were wedded. In the large cities, mention from the pulpit of eternal punishment, hell-fire, or the personal devil, evoke smiles and shrugs. To an unprejudiced observer it would appear that many of the old teachings have been left behind, never to return. But who knows, after all? Even their turn may come again.

Twenty-five years ago a close observer of the times would have felt perfectly safe in predicting that out of the bubbling pot of that day there must emerge the new teachings of materialism, which at that time seemed destined to carry the day. But alas for human prescience, the very reverse has happened. Materialism has been shown the door, for the time being, and, wonder upon wonders, advanced idealism has taken the center of the field of human philosophical thought. Yes, not only advanced idealism, but even a rarefied pantheism, under other names. The predictions of twenty-five years ago have proven false, and the tables have been turned on the prophets of that time. Materialism has been eliminated and its direct antithesis, idealistic pantheism, has been given the seat of honor. Not the crude materialistic pantheism which insists that Deity is but the total of natural objects and forces—but the spiritual phase of pantheism which insists that Deity is manifested in all natural things—the doctrine of the Immanent Spirit. And this even in its most idealistic sense, for the advance wave of modern philosophical thought certainly holds to the idea that the universe is in reality an idea or series of ideas in the universal mind. The most radical branch of the great Vedanta school of the Hindus, the Advaitists, have never dared to go farther in this direction than the most advanced adherents of the twentieth century idealism, which is exerting so powerful an influence on the public thought of to-day.

Some who have not as yet dared to go to the full length of this extreme idealism do not hesitate to teach and preach the full doctrine of the immanent Deity, which they hold is also taught by the Biblical teacher who said that "In Him we live and move and have our being." This surely is a most radical departure from the old teaching of the Deity who ever dwelt apart from His creation, and who made the universe from nothing. And surely, the standard built upon this new teaching must differ materially from those erected upon the old. It is this marked shifting of the foundation conception of the fundamental principles that has disturbed the edifice of thought, life and action to-day.

Have we discarded the solid rock for the sinking sand, or *vice versa?* Each must answer according to his own views and conceptions. The newer school claims that it has found solid rock at last; while the older school insists that its opponents are blasting at the Rock of Ages. Which is right—and "what shall the harvest be?" Time alone can answer. Each must be judged by its works. "By their fruits shall ye know them." And time is required for the fruits and works of the new. Perhaps from the old and the new, a still newer something may arise, better and nobler than either. Time must answer. Like the Sphinx, Time crouches on her haunches, and with pensive, undisturbed eyes gazes out into the eternity of the future. What does she see there—what does she see? Ah, if we could only know!

Those who may imagine that I have laid too much stress upon the popularity of the conceptions of the immanent Deity, or the Oneness of All, which is a distinctive feature of the newer thought of the day, I refer to the news columns of the papers of any large city in the land, containing the reports of the sermons delivered in the leading pulpits. Let them refer to the utterances of the great theological teachers of the day. Let them refer to the teachings of the following representative men of the great universities of the land, as reported in the daily press and magazines of the day. Surely these tell the tale in no uncertain tones.

Harold Bolce, in a recent article in the *Cosmopolitan Magazine*, entitled "Avatars of the Almighty," gives a number of instances in which college professors are teaching this new conception of fundamental principles—the conception of the indwelling Deity—of the immanent God. In conclusion, he states:

"And now that man has discovered that there resides in his nature a spirit or energy that is divine, the colleges say, and that

he can summon it to work his will, the potency and future operation of this psychic force no man can compute. Science has found a way through psychology to God; the opportunities for the race, through invoking in the human consciousness the brooding spirit that fills all space, are absolutely infinite. Science, therefore, is demonstrating along new lines, or at least is claiming to demonstrate, *that man is God made manifest.* And modern philosophy, as set forth in American universities, holds this incarnation not as a fanciful and merely beautiful ideal, but as a working and understandable principle in the soul of humanity. The professors, therefore, who are digging what they believe to be the graves for dead dogmas, stand as exponents of the teaching that *man is the embodiment and conscious expression of the force that guides all life and holds all matter in its course.* Man has begun the cycle of that triumphal daring prophesied by ancient seers, and which appealed so potently to the imagination of Poe. Not merely in religious rhetoric, but in reality, the school men say, *is man the avatar of God.* The reference to Poe is accompanied by the following quotation from that poet: "Think that the sense of individual identity will be gradually merged in the general consciousness—that man, for example, ceasing imperceptibly to feel himself man, will at length attain that awfully triumphant epoch, *when he shall recognize his existence as that of Jehovah.*"

The editor of the *Cosmopolitan,* in commenting on the article in question, says:

"The college professors, in some cases, express doubt as to the practicability and judgment of their teachings. Will their propaganda cause a rejection of all solemn and religious authority, create a Robespierre, and erect a guillotine, with its concomitant tumbrels and blood-atonement? The professors say no. They assert that in this, the sanest of all ages, man thinks for himself, and the path they blaze for him leads to the realization that he himself is an avatar, and incarnation, of God. . . . The conflict between the colleges and the church discloses a movement of thought more significant, perhaps, to civilization than even the Renaissance. In its revolutionary character, and in its importance to mankind, the only world-wide movement that can be compared with it was that upheaval in the eighteenth century which led, through bloodshed, to democracy. . . . The claim of the colleges is that they are teaching a higher form of truth. They hold that '*the orthodox God has had his day.*' . . . They say that when the God of theology is utterly banished from human thought the reign of man will begin. . . . They say, as indicated, that this spiritual revolution will not end in a saturnalia of tumbrels and guillotines, for this is not an atheistic banishment of God and his holy angels, but is, on the contrary, the enthronement of a new Jehovah—*a God that has become conscious and potent in the human mind.*"

Outside of the pulpits and universities other influences are at work. In the first place, there is felt the great influence of that great wave of transcendental thought which swept over the country during the last century, of which Emerson was the chief exponent. The effect of Emerson's transcendentalism is most marked in the present unrest in thought and conception. His "Oversoul" forms the basis of a mystical religion which has brought comfort and peace to many a weary soul. The very essence of his teaching is, of course, the Oneness of All, and the Indwelling Spirit. The influence of Walt Whitman, Edward Carpenter and Browning has been felt in the general movement toward the Transcendental conception. Maeterlinck has also drawn the attention and interest of many toward the same or similar conceptions. People who have studied the German philosophers, particularly Hegel and Schopenhauer, in many cases find themselves attracted toward the teaching and conceptions of the present stage of idealism.

The influence of the Congress of Religions, at the time of the World's Fair in Chicago, has led people to take a new interest in the study of comparative religion, particularly in the religions of the Orient, nearly all of which are based upon some form of pantheistic or idealistic doctrine. The effect of Christian Science and of the various New Thought cults and schools has been to lead people's minds in the same general direction—toward the "recognition, realization and manifestation of the God in me." In fact, it would seem as if a thousand circumstances had conspired to bring modern thought to a point in which it must consider the New Idealism and the new presentation of the Immanent and Indwelling Spirit. The world seems to have turned its back upon orthodoxy, but at the same time has refused to entertain and accept the teachings of materialism, notwithstanding the predictions of the thinkers of the last century. It needs something to fill the place of the old ideas, which are being discarded, and the idea of the Indwelling Spirit—the Oneness of All, the Union with God—appears to be the logical conception under all the circumstances. At the present time there is certainly a wave setting in from all directions, tending ever toward centering the world's thought upon the old-new conception of fundamental principles. Whether it is permanent, or whether it will disappear in a reactionary movement, or whether it will evolve into something still higher and nearer to truth—these are the questions that observing men are asking each other to-day. It is indeed a wise man who can answer them.

And now for the immediate effects of this change of conceptions regarding the fundamental principles. What effect is it having upon the people of to-day? What is its influence upon other lines of thought? What effect is it exerting upon the great economic, sociological, ethical and moral movements of the day? How is the new conception working out in actual practice? These are important questions —let us consider them.

From the viewpoint of the unchanged, steadfast members of the old guard of orthodoxy, the new conceptions are pernicious in their effect, and can work naught but harm to the race. In the first place, say these good people. There is nothing new about the thing—it is as old as the race. This is undoubtedly true, for the same teachings, beliefs and conceptions which are now so popular may be found in the oldest of the world's philosophies and religions. India and ancient Greece are the fountain head of the basic ideas of the modern popular conceptions. In the Vedanta, in the teachings of Buddha, in the writings of Plato, Heraclitus, Democritus and the Stoic philosophers, may be found the principles of the popular thought of to-day. The cycle, or spiral, of human thought has brought the old philosophies to the front as new. But is the fact that a new thing is really old any real argument against it? Secondly, say these critics: It comes from heathen sources. True, also, but this is circular reasoning—the fact that an old philosopher, before the days of Christianity, happened to fail to be a Christian, is no argument against his truths. Nor is all truth, wisdom and virtue the especial property of Christian thinkers. If we were to discard all heathen knowledge, the world would be a heavy loser. Thirdly, say the critics: It is naught but pantheism. This may be so, but, notwithstanding the odium attached to the term by the orthodox churchman, pantheism has inspired some of the world's greatest minds. There are two kinds of pantheism, the first being that of the materialists, who hold that God is but the sum and substance of the natural forces and objects; the second being the view of the "god-drunken philosopher," Spinoza, who held that "God was in all, and all in God;" that nature and the universe was but a manifestation of God; and that "to define God is to deny Him."

To understand the charge of "pantheism" hurled at the old-new conception of the Oneness of All, by the orthodox critics, one must realize what the pantheism of Spinoza is, and to realize how different it is from the old pantheism of the materialists. The following quotation, from the "Encyclopædic Dictionary," states the matter briefly and clearly:

"The system of Spinoza has been described as atheism, as

pantheism, and as the most rigid monotheism, according as his cardinal teaching—that there is but one substance, God—has been interpreted. By substance, however, Spinoza meant the underlying reality and ever-living existence, and he chose for the epigraph of his *Ethics* the words of St. Paul: 'In him we live and move and have our being' (Acts xvii:28). God is for him the one principle, having thought and extension as two eternal and infinite attributes constituting its essence, of which attributes mind and matter are the necessary manifestations; and thus he solves the problem of the relation of the finite to the infinite. Everything is a form of the ever-living existence, the substance, God, which is, and is not, nature, with which He is no more to be confounded than the fountain with the rivulet, or eternity with time. God is *natura naturans*, nature is *natura naturata;* the one is the energy, the other the act. In the same way, he explains the union of the soul with the body. Man is but a mode of the divine existence; his mind a spark of the divine flame; his body a mode of the infinite existence."

Surely this comes very near to agreement with the twentieth century conception of the omnipresent spirit. If one is pantheism, the other must be also. We leave this subject in the hands of the respective schools.

Fourthly, say the orthodox critics: When we deny the personality of God, we deny His Being as God, and resolve Him into a mere principle—the principle of nature. This is another matter which may be safely left for the consideration of the theologians. It is too technical for discussion here. We must, however, mention the view of Schopenhauer, who taught the idea of a World-Spirit, which he called "The Will to Live." He said: "When we assert pantheism we deny the existence of a God;

when we identify God with nature, we really show God to the door." The contention of the orthodox that all the attributes, qualities and characteristics which orthodoxy attributes to the personal God disappear when the personality is denied, seems to be worthy of respectful consideration. And the new conceptions certainly do emphatically deny the personality of God, and certainly do regard him as a principle. Therefore, we may understand the cry of orthodoxy, that "they would take away Jehovah, and supplant Him by a shadowy Principle." But a university professor has said: "The view of God which conceives him as external to the human self is a view which dominates the lowest forms of religions." Just how much of the old qualities, characteristics and attributes of the personal God may be preserved when the personal conception is supplanted by an abstract principle, which must by its nature be absolute and devoid of qualities, characteristics and attributes, is a question for the philosophers to argue among themselves. We do not hazard an opinion—we are merely the reporter of the observed ideas in the public mind.

But, finally cry the orthodox critics: "If you deny the personal God, the inspiration of the scriptures, and the authority of the church you sweep away the very standards of religion, morality and laws of human conduct. You leave nothing but a recourse to utilitarian ethics and systems of morality, built upon the changing ideals of man, or of his supposed needs. Your standards change with the times. You destroy all standards and the rock crumbles beneath your feet." We think this objection worthy of thought. It must follow that if the authority of the scriptures and the church is denied then the standards resting upon this authority must likewise fall, and man must be driven to the erection of standards based upon his reason, judgment and experience, rather than upon the authority of the scriptures and the church. And here is where many careful observers see the immediate cause of much of the sociological, economic and ethical unrest, and shifting standards of to-day. These observers say that the race, now in the process of discarding the old authority, must lose its faith in the infallibility of the old standards, and is beginning to create new standards, based upon the needs, real or supposed, of the race; and this occasions much of the turmoil and bubbling in the great Melting Pot of Modern Thought.

People are inquiring why they should be bound to old forms when the authority for those forms have been discarded. They ask why they should attempt to live up to the old admonitions: "Submit myself to all my governors, teachers, spiritual pastors and masters; to order myself lowly and reverently to all my betters; . . . to do my duty in that state of life into which it shall please God to call me"—when the authority of the church which so enjoined these duties is in grave doubt. They ask: "The Ten Commandments denied as inspired —then what commandments shall we follow?" If the scriptures are not inspired what is the true rule of conduct and life? These are the questions that the plain people are asking. They are in a transition stage. They are revolting against the old rules of social life, economics, and the old morality, in many instances. They are disputing many venerable old ideas regarding property, social duties, relation of state and citizen, marriage, etc. The barriers down, they are thinking of building according to their wishes or requirements, rather than upon the *dicta* of churchmen and ancient prophets. All these things are bubbling in the pot, because of the changing conceptions of fundamental principles.

On the other hand, the advocate of the new conceptions answers that, while this is all true—that while the old standards are being destroyed and discarded—that man is also engaged in building up for the race a newer, saner and grander edifice of thought—a better, truer and stronger set of standards, based upon human needs, experience and requirements—that instead of following the arbitrary commands of dead prophets and teachers, or of antiquated and discarded creeds, the race will move on, inspired by the Indwelling Spirit of God made manifest as man, ever toward higher and nobler efforts

—toward higher and better things, following ever the idea embodied in the lines of Holmes:

> "Build thee more stately mansions, O my soul;
> As the swift seasons roll!
> Leave thy low and vaulted past!
> Let each new temple, nobler than the last,
> Shut thee from heaven with a dome more vast,
> Till thou at length are free,
> Leaving thine outgrown shell by life's unresting sea."

And, in the meantime, those of us who may feel confused at this process of tearing down and rebuilding—who feel the pang of letting go of the old, and the perplexity and confusion resulting from the attempt to adapt ourselves to the new—we who, though our faces and intellect be turned toward the future, still feel that our hearts are with the past—what is there for us to do but to proceed in our search with a positive faith, knowing that a constant and persistent desire for truth must inevitably lead us into the very light of truth?

Thus it has come about that in the consideration of the conflicting ideas, theories and conceptions presenting themselves for consideration at the bar of modern thought, there is a new school which is now making its claims heard, and which many think destined to occupy a prominent position on the stage of interest in the near future. This school has for its basic principle the idea that abstract truth is unknowable—that the mind of man is unable to grasp the idea of abstract principle, any more than it can grasp that of abstract air, abstract water, abstract stone, etc. It holds that man does not, and cannot, know "whence he comes; whither he goes; or what is the object of his existence." And that, therefore, his highest wisdom lies in accepting this fact, and then living in the here and now; accepting what good may come to his hand; discarding all questions incapable of definite answer; being kind and doing good wherever he can, not as a duty, but because of the evolving feeling of the Brotherhood of Man; and finally testing all statements of truth by the touchstone of utility—asking ever the questions: "What is it good for? How will it work? What can be done with it? Does it make good?" This class of thinkers show a preference for the pragmatic view of thought and life, which Professor James has so well stated as: "The attitude of looking away from first things, principles, categories, supposed necessities; and of looking toward last things, fruits, consequences, facts." After all, would it not be strange if the pragmatic method should prove to be the solution—should prove to be the test to be applied to the products of the melting pot—the final test of: How does it work out? What is it good for? What will it do for the race? How far does it make good?

Meanwhile the pot is bubbling, seething and sputtering. The crucible is heated to its fullest extent. Some of the thoughts and ideas placed therein we know to be true; concerning others, there is grave doubt; but what will be the new arrangement, the new system, the new application; in brief, what will be poured forth from the pot? The world is on tiptoe, watching, wondering.

CHAPTER III

THE TRANSCENDENTAL MOVEMENT

As another straw showing which way the philosophical wind is blowing, in these days of intellectual unrest, and as a corroboration of the statements made in the preceding chapters of this book, I ask that you consider the following quotations from the latest work of Professor William James, of Harvard University, which work is based upon a series of lectures upon the philosophical situation of the present day. It should be stated, however, that these quotations do not necessarily represent Professor James's own personal beliefs or opinions, but are merely expressions of his observations regarding the prevailing spirit of modern philosophical thought in the universities and among men of advanced education. Professor James says:

"Those of us who are sexagenarians have witnessed in our own persons one of those gradual mutations of intellectual climate, due to innumerable influences, that make the thought of a past generation seem as foreign to its successor as if it were the expression of a different race of men. The theological machinery that spoke so livingly to our ancestors, with its finite age of the world, its creation out of nothing, its judicial morality and eschatology, its relish for rewards and punishments, its treatment of God as an external contriver, an 'intelligent and moral governor,' sound as odd to most of us as if it were some outlandish savage religion."

Professor James then goes on to speak of the spirit of modern philosophical thought in the universities, as follows:

> "Dualistic theism is professed at all Catholic seats of learning, whereas it has of late years tended to disappear at our British and American universities, and to be replaced by *a monistic pantheism more or less disguised.* I have an impression that ever since T. H. Green's time absolute idealism has been decidedly in the ascendant at Oxford. It is in the ascendant at my own university of Harvard." Also: "Our contemporary mind having once for all grasped the possibility of a more intimate *weltanschauung,* the only opinion quite worthy of arresting our attention will fall within the general scope of what may roughly be called *the pantheistic field of vision,* the vision of God as the indwelling divine rather than the external creator, and of human life as part and parcel of that deep reality."

In the present chapter it is my purpose to consider one of the most direct and immediate of the innumerable influences to which is due the present "gradual mutation of intellectual climate, that makes the thought of a past generation seem as foreign to its successor as if it were the expression of a different race of men," as Professor James has so well stated. This direct and immediate influence of which I speak, which has had so much to do with the bubbling of the Crucible of Modern Thought, is the influence of the Transcendental Movement of New England of 1830-1850, and the influence of Emerson in particular. I feel justified in asserting that the present condition of spiritual unrest and the prevalence of monistic idealism, while having its original source far back in the past history of thought, nevertheless reached us through the direct channel of the great Transcendental Movement in New England in the first half of the last century, and largely through the individual channel of expression of Ralph Waldo Emerson. The lovers and admirers of Emerson have long claimed this, and the opponents of the movement are now beginning to recognize it. As one disgusted orthodox speaker recently said: *"Emerson is the fellow who is at the bottom of all this trouble. His pantheistic teachings are now bearing fruit."*

The beginnings of the Transcendental Movement in New England may be seen in the remarkable interest manifested by educated New Englanders, during the first twenty-five years of the nineteenth century, toward the classical literature of England and Germany. Previous to that time the influence of Locke and Bentham had been dominant in philosophical thought in this country. The theory of innate ideas was denied, and there was a decided tendency in favor of the utilitarian basis of ethics and morals. Protesting against this view, some of the American Unitarians advanced ideas which, even in that early day, were denominated the "new thought,," and declared their preference for the conception that man possessed innate ideas and also higher faculties transcending the senses and the ordinary understanding. These advocates of the earlier "new thought" felt that religion and morality had a higher source than ordinary reason, and must be placed in the category of revelations of the intuition of man, arising from the presence of the Indwelling Spirit.

The influence of Coleridge, Wordsworth, Herder, Goethe and others began to displace that of the old literary idols, and exerted a decided direction in the formation of the "new thought" which was supplanting the older philosophical conceptions. Coleridge taught the doctrine of a higher reason, or transcendental intuition, by which he held the advanced soul might exercise *an immediate perception* of things supersensible, and which was not a faculty or property of the mind, but rather the manifestation of the Indwelling Spirit, which latter was a spark from the Universal Spirit. He held that there was but One Spirit, which was shared in by all human beings; the Many being, in a sense, identical with the One. Wordsworth taught a poetical pantheism, with its conception of a nature animated by the Universal Spirit, and as Universal Mind manifested as Law and Order. The influence of Goethe and other German writers were in the same general trend—all pointed in the direction of a new pantheistic philosophy. A new interest was awakened in Plato, and the Neo-Platonists, and a demand was shown for the writing of the mystics and idealists of the past. In this fruitful soil, the roots of the New England Transcendental Movement found that nourishment which led to its rapid growth.

Transcendentalism has been defined, briefly, as "*the philosophical conception that there can be knowledge of transcendental elements, or matters wholly beyond the ordinary experience of the human mind.*" The term was used by Kant. As Wallace says: "Kant's philosophy describes itself as Transcendentalism. The word causes a shudder, and suggests things unutterable." Transcendentalism is diametrically opposed to the philosophical views which hold that all knowledge arises from sensation or experience, and is also opposed to the agnostic view that reality is unknowable. But the term itself has taken on a wider and more general signification by reason of its popular use by the New England Transcendentalists, and its identification with the philosophy of Emerson, in the popular mind. In fact, the English-speaking peoples now use the word generally in the sense of designating the ideas and principles of the New England School, rather than those of the Kantian philosophy.

Margaret Fuller, one of the prominent New England Transcendentalists, in her "Memoirs," says:

"Transcendentalism was an assertion of the inalienable integrity of man; of the immanence of Divinity in instinct. . . . On the somewhat stunted stock of Unitarianism, whose characteristic dogma was trust in human reason, as correlative to Supreme Wisdom, had been grafted German Idealism, as taught by masters of most various schools—by Kant and Jacobi, Fichte and Novalis, Schelling and Hegel, Schleiermacher and de Wette, by Madam de Stael, Cousin, Coleridge, and Carlyle; and the result was a vague, yet exalting, conception of the god-like nature of the human spirit,

Transcendentalism, as viewed by its disciples, was a pilgrimage from the idolatrous world of creeds and rituals to the Temple of the Living God in the soul."

Herzog gives us the orthodox view of the philosophy, in his "Religious Encyclopedia," as follows:

"In religion, the typical Transcendentalist might be a sublimated theist; he was not, in any accepted sense, a Christian. He believed in no devil, in no hell, in no evil, in no dualism of any kind, in no spiritual authority, in no Savior, in no Church. He was humanitarian and an optimist. His faith had no backward look; its essence was aspiration, not contrition."

This last quotation is particularly interesting, inasmuch as it proves the contention of the influence of Transcendentalism upon the modern philosophical and religious thought. Compare Herzog's statements of what the Transcendentalist did not believe, and what he did believe, with the prevailing spirit of religio-philosophical thought, and see how the criticism of Transcendentalism becomes the prophecy of the popular thought of the early twentieth century! Surely this is a clear case of cause and effect.

About 1830, and the years immediately following, the various elements from which the Transcendental Movement was afterward composed began to approach each other, drawn together by the attraction of common interest. Emerson's "Nature," written in 1836, was an active element in the crystallization, although the writings of others had much to do with the amalgamation. These several books were so closely identified in their general philosophies and tendencies, that their readers began to form a loosely connected cult. Channing and Ripley, both prominent in Unitarianism and the "new thought" of the day, finally got together and formed a society for mutual endeavor and philosophical inquiry. Emerson, Margaret Fuller, Channing, Ripley, Brownson and Hedge, all prominent in the general movement, met and discussed the formation of a society. The term "Transcendentalism" was then first applied to the movement. Emerson says of this: "Nobody knows who first applied the name." The society was first called "The Symposium" and afterward "The Transcendental Club." Among the general subjects forming part of the earlier discussions were those of "Pantheism" and "Mysticism," respectively. The interest in the movement grew rapidly, and many of the brightest minds in New England were attracted to it. While the subjects discussed, taught and considered were various, it is safe to say that as a whole they were most unorthodox and contrary to the general public belief and opinion. Many of the ideas and opinions so advanced are quite familiar to the people of the present day, and are taught in many pulpits, but at the time of the Transcendental Movement they were regarded as heretical and atheistic, and aroused the fiercest denunciation and antagonism from the orthodox pulpit and press.

The formation of the Brook Farm Community at West Roxbury, Mass., by George Ripley, in 1841, is a part of the history of Transcendentalism, for the reason that some of the leading lights in the latter movement became members of the new community. Men like Ripley, Hawthorne, Alcott, Curtis, Channing and Dana, and women like Margaret Fuller, added a brilliancy to the Brook Farm Community, which has given it a prominent place in the history of the general movement. The aim of the community, as stated by one of their number, was "more effectually to promote the great purposes of human culture, to establish the external relations of life on the basis of wisdom and purity." The community flourished for a number of years, but like all such attempts, finally failed, the members dispersing, but carrying the spirit of the community with them in many directions.

In 1840, the publication of "The Dial" began. This was the organ of New England Transcendentalism, and naturally served to bring the movement into still more general notice and popularity. Margaret Fuller was the first editor, and Emerson, Channing, Alcott, Theodore Parker, Ripley, and Thoreau were among the contributors to the first number. Emerson wrote the opening article, entitled: "The Editors to the Reader." During the first two years of the existence of "The Dial" Margaret Fuller was assisted in her editorial work by Ripley and Emerson. After that time Emerson became the sole editor. Much that was crude and fanciful appeared in the pages of this publication, but also much that will hold a permanent place in the history of American literature. It marked an era in the history of American magazines, and gave an impetus, the effects of which are still noticeable. After four years of struggle it was finally discontinued.

The life of the Transcendental Movement may be said to be embraced by the years 1830 and 1850, although the beginnings were still further back in the century, and the influence of the movement still lives as the heart and spirit of many modern schools of thought and activity which are slow to acknowledge their indebtedness to it. Its real source was the great awakening of nearly a century before its time, in which the hold of Calvinism was rudely shaken and weakened, and which brought to the New England mind a new interest in Arminianism and Arianism, and which served to prepare the cradle for Unitarianism, which was afterward born. Transcendentalism was the natural spiritual child of the great spiritual unrest which had preceded it by about a century, and which wrought a great change in religious and philosophical thought and ideals in New England, which section at that time undoubtedly was the intellectual center of this country. It was the offspring of liberal Christian thought, combined with Neo-Platonism, Oriental Religions, and Occult Philosophy. It was perhaps nearer akin to what philosophy calls "Mysticism" than to any other one form of thought.

The spirit of Transcendentalism was most elusive, as all writers have remarked. The current impression at the present time may be stated in a quotation from Professors McGilvery and Trent, in their article on the subject in the "New International Encyclopedia," as follows:

> "It is difficult to disengage the elements, to delimit it in point of time, to say what it really accomplished, to determine what it became. . . . The era of the Transcendentalists was in many respects an American Renaissance, the effects of which were not confined to this country, but were spread chiefly through the writings of Emerson, Thoreau and Channing, to England, and to some extent to the Continent of Europe. That their ideas were vague anl often transcended reason, not to say common sense, that their literary work was largely amateurish, that their extravagances gave much occasion to legitimate ridicule, that their so-called movement was *the forerunner of religious and social manias of all sorts,* can scarcely be gainsaid; but it is equally idle to deny the loftiness of their aims and the importance of their work."

Be one's opinion of Transcendentalism what it may, no careful student of the Transcendental Movement can doubt the fact that in it may be found the underlying and immediate causes of the modern effects, manifested as the "New Thought" movement, on the one hand, and the tendency toward Monistic Idealism, or pantheism, evidenced in the philosophical thought of to-day, on the other hand. While it is true that the real causes of these later movements must be sought for still further back in the history of human thought, it cannot be doubted that the older impulses reached the present movements through the direct channel of the Transcendentalism of New England. An examination of the teachings and writings of that school, when compared with those of the later schools, shows a direct chain or sequence and of cause and effect. Those who are looking for the causes of the modern schools of thought will fail to find them unless they take into active consideration the Transcendental Movement of New England, of 1830-1850. And not only is this true, but it will be found that many other and apparently unrelated schools of thought arose about the same time, not entirely in sympathy with the general movement, but apparently arising from the influence thereof. Some of these side schools have their modern successors, tracing descent in a direct line. So that the influence of Transcendentalism in New England may be considered *the one vital factor* which has brought about that state of affairs which has resulted in the old conceptions sounding "as odd to most of us as if it were some outlandish savage religion," as Professor James has said; and in making possible the statement of the same careful authority that "the only opinion quite worthy of arresting our attention will fall within the general scope of what may roughly be called the pantheistic field of vision, the vision of God as the indwelling divine, rather than the external creator, and of human life as part and parcel of that great reality." Transcendentalism is the direct and immediate cause of this state of affairs. And Ralph Waldo Emerson is recognized as the fullest and clearest expression of Transcendentalism. As the orthodox speaker previously quoted said: "Emerson is the fellow who is at the bottom of all this trouble." Then let us see what Emerson really taught, and what he stood for. This will help to show us the connection between 1830-1850 and 1909.

CHAPTER IV

EMERSON, THE TORCH-BEARER

I shall not attempt to present, even briefly, an account of the life and work of Emerson. The facts regarding the man and his work have been told, and retold, by far abler pens. The libraries contain many books giving this information from the viewpoints of their respective writers. The encyclopedias give full accounts, more or less impartial, regarding the career of this brilliant star which blazed in the firmament of thought, and which, although it has been resolved into its original elements, still serves to brighten the minds and lives of men to-day, and will serve a like purpose for many generations to come. For our present purpose it is sufficient to consider the philosophy of the man only in its relation to, and connection with, the spirit of the thought of to-day which so many think has risen suddenly without an especial cause. As Plato says: "The problem of philosophy is, for all that exists conditionally, to find a ground unconditioned and absolute." From his first notable work, entitled "Nature," Emerson sought to establish his idea regarding that "ground unconditioned and absolute."

In considering the philosophy of Emerson, one

must not expect him to proceed, as have the majority of other philosophers, by scientific and logical reasoning—his method is rather intuitional than rational, in the ordinary usage of the latter term. Trent says of him:

"Being himself a man of many intuitions, and of wonderful vigor in phrasing them, he is to be regarded as a prophet rather than as a philosopher. He sought to construct no system, but stood for *a constant idealistic impulse.* What he wrote was not based primarily on experience, nor did he ever write as the so-called man of the world. He is criticized for relying chiefly or altogether upon his intuitive consciousness, instead of submitting his generalization to the test of reason."

Emerson was essentially an idealist. Personally, he preferred the latter term to that of Transcendentalist, as which he was classed by the men of his day, and which causes his philosophy to be termed Transcendentalism. He said that the majority of people did not know what they meant by the latter term. He said, whilst in the midst of the work of the Transcendental Movement:

"What is popularly called Transcendentalism among us is *Idealism*—Idealism as it appears in 1842. . . . The Idealism of the present day acquired the name of Transcendentalism by the use of that term by Immanuel Kant of Konigsberg, who replied to the skeptical philosophy of Locke, which insisted that there was nothing in the intellect which was not previously in the experience of the senses, by showing that there was a very important class of ideas, or imperative forms, which did not come by experience, but through which experience was acquired; that these were *intuitions* of the mind itself; and he denominated them *Transcendental* forms. The extraordinary profoundness and precision of that man's thinking have given vogue to his nomenclature, in Europe and America to that extent, *that whatever belongs to the class of intuitive thought is popularly called at the present day, Transcendental.*"

Emerson makes the following distinction and definition of Idealism:

"As thinkers, mankind have ever divided into two sects, Materialists and Idealists; the first class founded on experience, the second on consciousness; they perceive that the senses are not final; they give us representations of things, but what the things themselves are they cannot tell. The Materialist insists upon facts, on history, on the force of circumstances, and the animal wants of man; the Idealist, on the power of Thought and of Will, on inspiration, on miracle, on individual culture. The Idealist concedes all that the other affirms . . . and then asks him for his grounds of assurance that things are as his senses represent them. But, I, he says, affirm facts not affected by the illusions of sense, facts which are of the same nature as the faculty which reports them. . . . He does not deny the sensuous fact—by no means; but he will not see that alone."

This definition recalls the celebrated classification of Prof. William James, who, in his work on "Pragmatism," says:

"I will write these traits down in two columns. I think you will practically recognize the two types of mental make-up that I mean if I head the columns by the titles 'tender-minded' and 'tough-mindel,' respectively:

"THE TENDER-MINDED	"THE TOUGH-MINDED
Rationalistic (going by 'principles'),	Empiricist (going by 'facts'),
Intellectualistic,	Sensationalistic,
Idealistic,	Materialistic,
Optimistic,	Pessimistic,
Religious,	Irreligious,
Free-Willist,	Fatalistic,
Monistic,	Pluralistic,
Dogmatical."	Skeptical."

"Each of you probably knows some well-marked example of each type, and you know what each example thinks of the example on the other side of the line. They have a low opinion of each other. Their antagonism, whenever as individuals their temperaments have been intense, has formed in all ages a part of the philosophic atmosphere of the time. It forms a part of the philosophic atmosphere of to-day. The tough think of the tender as sentimentalists and soft-heads. The tender feel the tough to be unrefined, callous and brutal. Their mutual reaction is very much like that that takes place when Boston tourists mingle with a population like that of Cripple Creek. Each side believes the other to be inferior to itself; but disdain in one case is mingled with amusement, in the other it has a dash of fear."

There is no doubt regarding the place to which Emerson must be assigned in the classification given by Professor James. He is the ideal "tender-minded" individual. He is an idealist of the idealists. As Cooke says:

"Emerson belongs in the succession of the Idealists. That company he loves wherever its members are found, whether among Buddhists or Christian mystics, whether Transcendentalist or Sufi, whether Saadi, Boehme, Fichte, or Carlyle. These are the writers he studies, these the men he quotes, these the thinkers who come nearest his own thought. He is in the succession of minds who have followed in the wake of Plato, who is regarded by him as the world's greatest thinker. More directly still, Emerson is in that succession of thinkers represented by Plotinus, Eckhardt and Schelling, who have interpreted Idealism in the form of Mysticism."

Whipple says of Emerson as a philosopher:

"His intellect is intuitive, but not reflective. It contains no considerable portion of the element which is essential to the philosopher. His ideas *proceed from the light of genius*, and from wise observation of Nature; they come *in flashes of inspiration and ecstasy;* his pure gold is found in places near the surface, not brought out laboriously from the depths of the mine in the bowels of the earth. He has no taste for the apparently arid abstractions of philosophy. His mind is not organized for the comprehension of its sharp distinctions. Its acute reasonings present no charm to his fancy, and its lucid deductions are to him as destitute of fruit as an empty nest of boxes. In the sphere of pure speculation he has shown neither originality nor depth. He has thrown no light on the great topics of speculation. He has never fairly grappled with the metaphysical problems which have called for the noblest efforts of the mind in every age, and which, not yet reduced to positive science, have not ceased to enlist the clearest and strongest intellects in the work of their solution. On all questions of this kind the writings of Emerson are wholly unsatisfactory. He looks at them *only in the light of the imagination.* He frequently offers brave hints, pregnant suggestions, cheering encouragements, but no exposition of abstract truth has ever fallen from his keen pen."

As a philosopher, Emerson belongs to that class of geniuses who may be termed intuitional, inspirational, awakening, stimulating. As Cooke well says of him: "Emerson belongs to that company of illuminated souls who have done for the modern world what the sages, prophets and seers did for the ancient world." He is a Hindu *guru*, or a Sufi *pir*, rather than a Western teacher. He disdains the necessity of proof, and feels that his words should carry their own proof. His is the attitude of the sage of the Orient, rather than of the professor of philosophy of the Western world.

That Emerson's thought is based upon that of Plato and the Neo-Platonists cannot be doubted, although there always appears running through his mental creations the golden thread of the teachings of Oriental thought. Plato would claim him as a son

—the Hindu Vedantist and the Persian Sufi would claim him as a brother. Mystics of every age, and of every land, would welcome him as of their own kind. Believers in reincarnation would attribute to him successive births first in Hindu and in Persian bodies, and later in the fleshly garments of philosophers of ancient Greece. He is of the royal mystic descent, in a straight and unbroken line. His "Over-Soul" might have been written either by a Hindu Vedantist, a Persian Sufi, or a "god-drunken" Grecian philosopher. Modern advocates of what is called "cosmic consciousness" find an explanation for his genius in their theories, and, indeed, in his "Over-Soul" he gives utterances that would indicate an experience of the kind indicated by this school.

Emerson holds that God is the Universal Substance, from which the universe is formed; the Universal Mind which holds the mind of all; the Universal Spirit which is immanent in all men. He says:

"There seems to be a necessity in Spirit to manifest itself in material forms; and day and night, river and storm, beast and bird, acid and alkali pre-exist in necessary Ideas in the mind of God, and are what they are by virtue of preceding affections in the world of Spirit." . . . "The world proceeds from the same Spirit as the body of man. It is a remoter and inferior incarnation of God, a projection of God in the unconscious." . . . "Under all this running sea of circumstance, whose waters ebb and flow with perfect balance, lies the original abyss of real Being. Essence, or God, is not a relation, or a part, but the whole. Being is the vast affirmative, excluding negation, self-balanced, and swallowing up all relations, parts, and times within itself . . . on every topic is the resolution of all into the everlasting One."

To Emerson, God is all in All, and All in all. He says:

> "Truth, goodness and beauty are but different faces of the same All. . . . God *is*, and all things are but shadows of him." . . . "The true doctrine of omnipresence is, that God reappears with all His parts in every moss and cobweb. The value of the universal contrives to throw itself into every point."

But Emerson does not try to define God. Like Spinoza, he holds that "to define God is to deny him." He says:

> "Of that ineffable essence which we call Spirit, he that thinks most will say least." . . . "We can forsee God in the coarse, and, as it were, distant phenomena of matter, but when we try to define and describe himself, both language and thought desert us, and we are helpless as fools and savages. That essence refuses to be recorded in propositions; but when man has worshiped intellectually, the noblest ministry of nature is to stand as the apparition of God. It is the organ through which the universal spirit speaks to the individual, and strives to lead back the individual to it."

He sings:

> "Thou meetest him by centuries,
> And lo! he passes like the breeze;
> Thou seek'st in globe and galaxy,
> He hides in pure transparency;
> Thou askest in fountains and in fires,
> He is the essence that inquires.
> He is the axis of the star;
> He is the sparkle of the spar;
> He is the heart of every creature;
> He is the meaning of each feature;
> And his mind is the sky,
> Than all it holds more deep, more high."

His poem, "Brahma," voices the true Oriental spirit:

> "If the red slayer thinks he slays,
> Or if the slain thinks he is slain,
> They know not well the subtle ways
> I keep, and pass, and turn again.
> Far or forgot to me is near;
> Shadow or sunlight are the same;
> The vanished gods to me appear;
> And one to me are shame or fame.
> They reckon ill who leave me out;
> When they fly, I am the wings;
> I am the doubter and the doubt,
> And I the hymn the Brahmin sings.
> The strong gods pine for my abode,
> And pine in vain the Sacred Seven;
> But thou, meek lover of the good!
> Find me, and turn thy back on heaven."

To Emerson, God is not a far-away Deity, but immanent Being. Emerson might have written the very words of Goethe, when the latter says:

> "What kind of God was he who impelled things only from outside, and let the universe twirl around his fingers? God moves the world inwardly, cherishes nature in himself, himself in nature, so that whatever lives and works and exists in him never misses his power nor his spirit."

It formerly was the fashion to defend Emerson from the charge of pantheism, because that term was misunderstood, or understood only in one of its senses. Theodore Parker once wrote regarding Emerson: "He has absolute confidence in God. He has been foolishly accused of pantheism, which sinks God in Nature; but no man is further from it." But

Emerson is a pantheist, in the usage of the term which indicates that God is immanent in His nature, and that all substance is of the One Substance; all mind of the One Mind; all spirit of the One Spirit. His, indeed, is the forerunner of the teaching of to-day, which, as Professor James has said, "may roughly be called *the pantheistic field of vision, the vision of God as the indwelling divine rather than the external creator, and of human life as part and parcel of that deep reality.*" No one who reads his "Nature" and his "Over-Soul" can have any doubts as to Emerson's true position regarding true pantheism, nor his being the direct inspiration of the modern trend of thought in that direction.

Emerson taught that there exists a great World-Spirit—the Over-Soul in which we live and move and have our being. He says:

"The Supreme critic on all the errors of the past and present, and the only prophet of that which must be, is that great nature in which we rest as the earth lies in the soft arms of the atmosphere; that Unity, that Over-Soul, within which every man's particular being is contained and made one with all other; that common heart of which all sincere conversation is the worship, to which all right action is submission; that overpowering reality which confutes our tricks and talents, and constrains everyone to pass for what he is, and to speak from his character and not from his tongue, and which evermore tends to pass into our thought and hand and becomes wisdom and virtue and power and beauty. We live in succession, in division, in parts, in particles. Meantime, within man is the soul of the whole; the wise silence; the universal beauty; to which every part and particle is equally related; the Eternal One. . . . We see the world piece by piece, as the sun, the moon, the animal, the tree; but the whole, of which these are shining parts, is the soul."

He holds that the individual soul may, and does, hold communion with the Over-Soul. He says:

"The heart which abandons itself to the Supreme Mind finds itself related to all its works, and will travel a royal road to particular knowledge and powers. For in ascending to this primary and aboriginal sentiment we have come from our remote station on the circumference instantaneously to the center of the world, where . . . we see causes, and anticipate the universe, which is but a slow effect. This communication is an influx of the Divine Mind into our mind. It is an ebb of the individual rivulet before the flowing surges of the sea of life. Every distinct apprehension of this central commandment agitates men with awe and delight. A thrill passes through all men at the reception of a new truth, or at the performance of a great action, which comes out of the heart of nature. In these communications the power to see is not separated from the will to do, but the insight proceeds from obedience, and the obedience proceeds from a joyful perception. Every moment when the individual feels himself invaded by it, it is memorable. Always, I believe, by the necessity of our constitution a certain enthusiasm attends the individual consciousness of that divine presence. The character and duration of this enthusiasm varies with the state of the individual, from an ecstacy and trance and prophetic inspiration,—which is its rarer appearance, to the faintest glow of virtuous emotion, in which form it warms, like our household fires, all the families and associations of men, and makes society possible. . . . The trances of Socrates; the 'union' of Plotinus; the vision of Porphyry; the convulsions of George Fox and his Quakers; the illumination of Swedenborg, are of this kind. What was in the case of these remarkable persons a ravishment, has, in innumerable instances in common life, been exhibited in less striking manner. Everywhere the history of religion betrays a tendency to enthusiasm. The raptures of the Moravian and Quietist; the opening of the internal sense of the Word, in the language of the New Jerusalem Church; the revival of the Calvinistic churches; the experiences of the Methodists, are varying forms of that shudder of awe and delight with which the individual soul always mingles with the universal soul. The nature of these revelations is always the same; they are perceptions of the absolute law. They are solutions of the soul's own questions. They do not answer the questions which the understanding asks. The soul answers never by words, but by the thing itself that is inquired after. . . . Behold, it saith, I am born into the great, the universal mind. I, the imperfect, adore my own Perfect. I am somehow receptive to the great soul, and thereby do I overlook the sun and the stars and feel them to be but the fair accidents and effects which change and pass. More and more the surges of everlasting nature enters into me, and I become public and human in my regards and actions. So come I to live in thoughts and act with energies which are immortal."

Emerson has much more to say of this communion with the Over-Soul. He agrees with the old mystics in holding that the "union with God" is possible, and even frequent. He teaches the attainment of "cosmic consciousness," by the power of contemplation and the silence. St. Theresa and Madame Guyon, Plotinus and Swedenborg, would have recognized him as a brother *illuminatus*. He speaks of the power of communion with the Over-Soul as "always a miracle, which no frequency of occurrence or incessant study can ever familiarize, but which must always leave the inquirer stupid with wonder." He says, in one of his essays:

"The path is difficult, secret, and beset with terror. The ancients called it ecstacy or absence—a getting out of their bodies to think. All religious history contains traces of the trance of saints—a beatitude, but without any sign of joy, earnest, solitary, even sad; the 'flight' Plotinus called it, 'of the alone to the alone;' the closing of the eyes—whence our word 'mystic.' . . . This beatitude comes in terror, and with shocks to the mind of the receiver."

These experiences are common in the writings of all the mystics, ancient and modern—it is their distinctive mark and sign. Undeterred by the unfeeling suggestion of modern material science that these strange experiences are pathological rather than spiritual—the result of overwrought emotions, rather than of the opening of spiritual faculties—the mystic ever clings to his transcendental experiences, and hold them to be the most real moments of his existence. The mystic smiles in a superior manner at the presumption of modern psychology which seeks to place these experiences in the category of the abnormal, rather than of the super-normal. He has *experienced*—and is content.

But, in the end, Emerson, like all of the Mystics, is compelled to report that he finds it impossible to express in words the experiences he wishes to describe. He confesses that repeatedly, but perhaps at no time more beautifully than when he declares: "Words from a man who speaks from that life, must sound vain to those who do not dwell in the same thought on their own part. I dare not speak for it. My words do not carry its august sense; they fall short and cold. Only itself can inspire whom it will, and behold; their speech shall be lyrical and sweet, and universal as the rising of the wind. Yet I desire, even by profane words, if sacred I may not use, to indicate the heaven of this deity, and to report what hints I have collected of the transcendent simplicity and energy of the Highest Law."

A careful examination and study of the Transcendental Movement of New England, of 1830-1850, especially as expressed through the writings of Emerson and more especially through his "Nature" and his "Over-Soul," will convince any fair-minded person that in this movement, and in this one writer, may be found *the direct and immediate channel* through which has come to us the popular philosophic spirit of the day; the trend of modern religious thought; and the fundamental principles of what has been called the "New Thought" in all of its philosophical and mystical phases. We may find Emerson voicing these "new" truths of to-day, in almost the very words used by the latter-day teachers and writers, many of whom seem unwilling to acknowledge his influence. Over the space of sixty to eighty years these teachings have traveled, and are now awakening into full vigor and power. As important elements in the bubbling and seething Crucible of Modern Thought, Transcendentalism and Emersonianism must be accorded first place. Someone has said that when we seek a cause, we are really seeking "something to put the blame on." In this case the cause and the blame must be placed upon Emerson and his band of earnest seekers after truth who formed the "Transcendental Club" in 1836, all of whom passed from the field of conflict without realizing the harvest which has resulted from their industrious seed-sowing. To them must be accorded the praise or the blame—according to one's particular viewpoint of the subject.

CHAPTER V

THE FOUNT OF ANCIENT GREECE

In the preceding chapter we considered the influence and direct effect of Transcendentalism, and of Emerson in particular upon modern popular thought. But behind Emerson and the Transcendental school there were many other influences, which we shall now proceed to consider in these articles. One of the great primary sources or causes of the modern trend of thought—that strange revival of old thought in new forms—is that of the philosophy of ancient Greece. Not alone does the present movement show the strong influence of the old Greek philosophical thought, but the Greek ideals are also to be found at the very heart of the "advanced" religious thought of to-day. The "New Theology" and the "New Religion" of which we hear so much contain many of the essential ideals of the ancient Greek religio-philosophic schools.

Wherever there has been a tendency toward transcendentalism, there we find the subtle but powerful influence of Neo-Platonism. And, so, in the great Transcendental Movement of New England, of which Emerson was the high priest, Neo-Platonism was the chief inspiration. Realizing the influence of Emerson and the Transcendental Movement on modern thought, we may see the important part played by the spirit of Neo-Platonism in supplying many of the leading ingredients to the Crucible of Modern Thought. The soul of this old school of thought persists in "marching on" throughout the centuries of thought, although its original body has long been "mouldering in the grave." Or, may we not say that its soul persists in "reincarnating" in new bodies, from time to time? It certainly seems to have taken on a new body of flesh of considerable size and strength in this first decade of the twentieth century.

In modern scientific Monism, we find a decided going back to Heraclitus, with his doctrine of "the universal flux;" of "everything Becoming and nothing Being;" of his conception of the ever changing, shifting, moving, universe of things, with its successive cycles. In Herbert Spencer, and other schools of modern scientific thought, we see the thought of Anaximander and Heraclitus revived. And in Spencer's conception of "The Infinite and Eternal Energy, from which all things proceed"—his "Unknowable"—we hear the distinct echo of the voices of the earliest thinkers of the older schools of ancient Greece. The spirit of Athens is walking abroad today in the great Universities of Europe and America—and many of the world's greatest minds are bidding her welcome to her new home. The broth that is being brewed in the great pot has a decided flavor of the Attic herb.

At the very heart of all Greek thought is the idea of a oneness, which is expressed as monism in philosophy, and as pantheism in the higher religious thought of the educated classes. One breathes the pantheistic atmosphere when he enters the enchanted realm of the old Greek thought. Mr. E. F. Benson, in his latest novel. "A Reaping," speaks of this subtle spirit of pantheism, which, while condemned in all orthodox religions, has nevertheless managed to creep in and make its home in the newer creeds, as it did in all the old ones, at the last. The following quotation will give Benson's conception of this subtle spirit of thought and belief:

"There is no myth that grew so close to the heart of things as the story of Pan, for it implies the central fact of all, the one fact that is so indisputably true, that all the perverted ingenuity of man has been unable to split into various creeds about it. For Pan is all, and to see Pan or hear him playing on his pipes means to have the whole truth of the world and the stars, and Him who, as if by a twisting thumb and finger, set them endlessly spinning through infinite space, suddenly made manifest. Flesh and blood, as the saying is, could not stand that, and there must be a bursting of the mortal envelope. Yet that, indisputably also, is but the cracking of the chrysalis. How we shall stand, weak-eyed still and quivering, when transported from the dusk in which we have lived this little life in the full radiance of the eternal day! How shall our eyes gain strength and our wings expansion and completeness, when the sun of which we have seen but the reflection and image is revealed? That is to see Pan. It killed the mortal body of Psyche—the soul—when she saw him on the hilltop by the river, and heard the notes of his reed float down to her; but she and every soul who has burst the flimsy

barrier of death into life joins in his music, and every day makes it the more compelling. Drop by drop the ocean of life, made up of the lives that have been, rises in the bowl in which God dips His hands. He touches every drop."

In both modern pantheism and modern idealism, the influence of the ancient Greek great masters of thought may be plainly discerned. In fact, the modern thought along these lines flows in a direct and unbroken course from the fountains of ancient Greece. While, as we shall see in another chapter, the seeds of all forms of philosophical and religious thought may be found in the early teachings of India and other Oriental lands, still we may regard the schools of philosophy of ancient Greece as the direct source of the fundamental conceptions and ideas which are now experiencing a remarkable revival in popularity and general acceptance. As Prof. John Dewey has said: "The Eleatic school may be regarded as the forerunners of pantheism in their insistence upon the unity and all comprehensiveness of true being. The distinction between finite and infinite, God and the world, had not, however, been made sufficiently clear at this time to justify calling the system pantheism. Through Plato and Aristotle the terms of the problem, both in themselves and in their relation to each other, are made evident. Neo-Platonism and Stoicism are both pantheistic. The former is of a logical, idealistic type, based upon Plato's theory of the relation between the One Being, *Nous*, and the Ideas; teaching that the world is simply one of a series of emanations from God, radiating from Him, as light from the sun, and having its apparent distinction only through a negative element, Non-Being or Matter." And, as Prof. A. S. Pringle-Pattison has said: "The first historical system to which the name of Idealism is applied by common consent is that of Plato. . . . The Idealistic system might be fitly styled the Platonico-Aristotelian."

PRE-SOCRATIC SCHOOLS

The Pre-Socratic schools of ancient Greece, which flourished about five hundred years before the Christian era, endeavored to establish a unity or one reality behind the various phenomena of the universe. Rising above the primitive myths, they sought to establish a fundamental substance, of which all the world of appearance was by a manifestation or reflection. Even before their time, thinkers had assumed a fundamental oneness in Nature, and the Pre-Socratic schools endeavored to find out what this One was. Their first questions were, "What is the primal substance? From what does all come? What is the essence of things?" At first, the answers implied the fundamental nature of material substances. Thales thought that "water" was the answer; Anaximenes said, "air;" and Anaximander suggested a "boundless" or "infinite" something, somewhat resembling the modern scientific conception of the ether. Each of their three schools, however, regarded the fundamental substance as animate, and possessing all the qualities and attributes of life and mind.

HERACLITUS

Heraclitus, the Ephesian, (500 B. C.) advanced a newer and much more advanced conception. He held that the universal substance is an ethereal, spiritual essence, symbolized by fire—a living, moving, active principle, constantly manifesting change in form of manifestation. He considered this principle rather in its objective, than in its subjective phase—he held that instead of "being," it should be thought that "everything is becoming." Just as the flame is apparently constant, although its particles are constantly changing, so is the universal flame really more of a "becoming" than of a "being." He held that nothing is stable except instability—nothing constant but change. Everything is in a state of flux—everything begins to change the moment it is created or born. The law of change is ever manifesting itself. Nothing persists. Everything is in constant motion and subject to constant change. The flame evidently "desires" change, and abhors stability. Action and reaction—involution, evolution, and devolution—the laws of cycles and rhythms—an immutable law of change causing a beginningless and endless sequence cause and effect—these were the teachings of Heraclitus. His fire was not a material fire, but a spiritual flame. In many particulars his philosophy agrees with that of Herbert Spencer —across the chasm of nearly 2,500 years these two great thinkers clasp hands. The influence of Heraclitus upon the later Stoic schools was most marked —and through them he has influenced still later schools. The latest works of Western physical science make many a mention of the name of this old Ephesian thinker, whose name has almost become forgotten in the interval. His ideas, I think, will be found much in evidence in the philosophies of the future.

THE ELEATICS

The Eleatics, another school of this period, gave much consideration to the old problem concerning "the One and the Many," laying special emphasis upon "the One." Xenophanes was as eloquent and active as any modern Monist in denouncing the anthropomorphic conceptions of Deity, and said boldly that "the One is God—God is the One"—and thus made the first real pantheistic statement of the early Greek philosophy. In this identification of God with "the One," is found the basic thought of all pantheism, ancient and modern. Parmenides enlarged upon this idea of Oneness, holding that, "What is must always have been, and must always be. Change is impossible to the One, for that would imply that something could arise out of nothing, or pass into nothing, both of which suppositions are foreign to rational thought. He thus identified God with the Absolute.

THE PYTHAGOREANS

The Pythagoreans, in their earlier days at least, devoted less time to speculation than to religious and ethical thought, at least so far as their public utterances were concerned. In their inner circles, they taught a mystical doctrine, in which certain forms of idealistic pantheism undoubtedly had a part, although their conception seemed rather toward that of a transcendental law rather than toward Deity. Their teaching regarding the "mystic numbers," etc., is believed to have been identified with certain occult doctrines, probably acquired from Egypt and Chaldea. Anaxagorus held that above the atomic forms and ultimate elements, of which the universe was composed, there was the *Nous,* or Universal Principle of Law and Order, which acts intelligently in ordering the universe—the principle of mind in substance.

SOCRATES

The second great period of ancient Greek philosophical thought is that of the "Socratic Schools," which derive their name from their founder, Socrates, who lived 469-393 B. C. Socrates did not aim to found a school, and his teachings were expounded most publicly, but his followers established several schools in which his thought was held as fundamental truth. Socrates' influence upon modern thought is manifested principally through his disciples who came after him establishing great schools of thought, particularly Plato and Aristotle. His influence upon the Stoics was also marked, Epictetus frequently referring to him as authority.

The term "Socratic Philosophy," is generally used in the broad sense of indicating the developing Greek philosophy from the time of Socrates to the rise of the school of Neo-Platonism, because, with the exception of the Epicureans, the principal philosophical schools of that period were in the habit of basing their respective and varying systems upon the fundamental authority of Socrates. It is quite a difficult matter to pin Socrates down to any particular system or school of thought, because his range of thought was so wide, and his tastes so catholic, that he seemed to embrace all systems of philosophy within his general field of discussion. In fact, we know Socrates principally through the medium of his followers and their several schools of philosophy —chiefly through the writings of Xenophon, Plato and Aristotle. Socrates was rather *an inspirer of philosophical thought* than the founder of a school of philosophy.

As an authority says: "It was the custom of

Socrates to carry on his investigations from propositions generally received as true, and to place the particular statement to be examined in a variety of combinations, thus implying that each thought must, if true, maintain its validity under every possible combination. . . . This method was employed by its author in the form of dialogue, from which arose the term, the Socratic Method. . . . All previous philosophers had been occupied with the universe as a whole; the chief business of Socrates was with man as a moral being. Bishop Bloomfield says: "Socrates taught that the divine attributes might be inferred from the works of creation. He maintained the omniscience, ubiquity, and providence of the Deity; and from the existence of conscience in the human breast he inferred that man is a moral agent, the object of reward and punishment; and that the great distinction of virtue and vice was ordained by Deity."

PLATO

Plato, by many considered the greatest philosopher of ancient Greece, lived from 429 to 348 B. C. He was the founder of the famous Academic school of philosophy. His influence over the thought of his time was very great, and it extended long after his time, influencing the great Neo-Platonic school, and having much to do with the formation of many conceptions in the early Christian Church. His influence, through the channel of Neo-Platonism, reached Emerson and the Transcendental Movement, hundreds of years later, as we saw in a recent chapter, and many of his ideas are now in evidence in the advanced thought of the twentieth century.

Lewes, in his "History of Philosophy," says of Plato: "I come to the conclusion that he never systemized his thoughts, but allowed free play to skepticism, taking opposite sides in every debate, because he had no steady conviction to guide him, unsaying to-day what he said yesterday, satisfied to show the weakness of an opponent." But other authorities see in this apparent shifting attitude of Plato rather a desire to consider all sides and phases of each and every question under discussion, in order to arrive at the whole truth. There were certain fundamental theoretical views held and taught by Plato which appear in his writings, and which are likened to the golden thread upon which the varied beads of his general thought are strung. These fundamental theories are as follows: (1) The existence of Ideas; (2) the doctrine of Pre-existence and Immortality of the Soul; and (3) the subjection of the popular divinities to the one Supreme Being.

The Platonic Doctrine of Ideas embodies the fundamental conception of idealism which has since played an important part in the shifting conceptions of the various schools of philosophical thought. Plato's idealism was the first Western presentation of the underlying principle of that school of thought. "Idealism" is the term applied in metaphysics to any theory which holds that the universe, as a whole, and throughout, is the embodiment of mind—that reality is to be found only in mind, and that the only reality in the external world consists in its perceptibility. Larousse says: "Idealism is the name given to certain systems which deny the individual existence of object apart from subject, or of both apart from God or the Absolute." Another authority says: "Idealism denies the existence of bodies, holding that their appearances are merely ideas of the subject cognized. Subjective idealism holds that these ideas are produced by the mind; while objective idealism holds that they exist only in God or the Absolute. Zeno, or Elea, in classic times, anticipated modern idealism. His teachings were subject to many changes, finally appearing in the refined conception of Plato, which in turn was modified by modern schools of idealistic thought."

Plato held that reality inhered in the general idea of a thing, and not in the individual; that there was no reality in the individual, tree, stone or man, but that reality was to be found in the general idea of tree, stone or man, which existed on the ideal plane alone. The essence or ideal form of things was held to be the only real thing; the objects of phenomenal appearance being merely fleeting, perishable copies of the real form or idea, the latter existing and being in a state of changeless unity eternally. These real ideas, forms or essences, existed on a plane of their own, and could be described only by metaphors. Plato's Ideal World was a realm of pure mind possessing substance and power. Reality could not be discovered by the ordinary mental process, but "The soul discovers the universal of things by herself." The true home of the soul was in the world of the "universals"—of the changeless ideas—separate and apart from sensations and individual mind.

Plato held that the world of phenomena lacked reality, as all reality is vested in the Noumenon, which is reality itself—the Noumenon is the cause and mover of all things, ever behind the veil of the senses and mortal mind. This Noumenon is that which all philosophies that acknowledge an Absolute are compelled to postulate as being. It was to be known only through pure thought, or intuition, rather than by the ordinary intellectual faculties. It had as its essence the Nous, an immaterial principle of pure mind, the reason and cause of the universe. The Nous is also considered as the Supreme Good, the source of all end and aims, and the supreme principle of all the ideas. The Nous was held to be transcendent, moving the world only as a rational immanent causer. It was Being, itself—the Absolute.

Plato also held that all true knowledge arises from the recollection or reminiscences of the soul, which has lived before, and has dwelt awhile on the transcendental plane of the ideas. The soul has perceived these ideas on that plane, and remembers them faintly in its subsequent earth life. As Wordsworth said: "Our birth is but a sleep and a forgetting." True knowledge and wisdom, Plato held, are but more or less dim recollections of the previously known Ideas, awakened by the associations, suggestions and experiences of earth life—by the imperfect copies of the Idea seen therein. He held that some Ideas, firmly implanted in the soul in the form of transcendent memories, can not be fully perceived in earth life, but always remain as idealistic dreams, toward the realization of which the soul intuitively yearns. Among these unexpressed ideas were "the Good, the Beautiful, and the True," all of which are incapable of expression, but which are recognized by the soul as real, and which awaken ecstatic thrills when contemplated. The earth-bound souls experience the ecstasy of transcendental memories—the recollection of the beatific visions of the past world of Ideas. The plane or world of ideas represent absolute wisdom, absolute being, absolute bliss.

Plato did not attempt to define his conception of Transcendent Being—wisdom—bliss—his absolute Nous. Like Spinoza, centuries afterward, he felt that "to define God is to deny Him," and he confined himself to metaphors and abstract terms. He regarded the phenomenal universe as but an appearance, mode, aspect, limitation, or aspect of the One Absolute Being which was above human thought or mortal mind; and this universe, being what it was, had no separate or real existence apart from that One Being. An authority speaks of "Plato's conception of the Nous, or One Absolute Being, from whom emanated as radiations all the phenomenal universe, which was made apparent only through the medium of an element of negation, or non-being, which men called matter."

ARISTOTLE

Aristotle (384-322 B. C.) is generally thought of as opposing Plato's philosophy, because of his substitution of his own terms, and because of his difference of interpretation of certain doctrines. While he did not agree with Plato upon some points, yet the two channels of Socratic thought were closely allied. Aristotle was a man of marvelous intellect, and he exerted a tremendous influence upon both ancient and modern philosophical and scientific thought. He joined Plato's school, and dwelt in Athens for twenty years. He was the tutor of Alexander the Great; a distinguished scholar; a great teacher. As an authority says: "Aristotle was the author of treatises on nearly every subject of human thought, and the founder of the Peripatetic philosophy, his writings on that theme and on Logic being venerated during the Middle Ages as no other book was but the Bible." Through Aristotle, Plato's fundamental thought concerning the Nous strongly influenced the Stoic schools, and from them descended through various channels to the present day.

Plato reaches the present day through various channels, many of which are now meeting for the first time since their original separation. The twentieth century crucible of thought has many ingredients coming direct from Plato's brain, though reaching the melting pot from several sources apparently opposed to each other. His pantheism comes to us through one channel; his idealism through another. And lo! meeting in the Western world, in the twentieth century, they assert their original unity by flying toward each other, in complete harmony and unity, just as two separated atoms of an element seek each other's embrace. It is common among students of idealism and transcendentalism, when considering the origin of a leading thought, to close the discussion by saying: "You will find it all said by Plato;" or "Plato includes all original thought on the subject." Such is the influence of Plato on modern thought.

CHAPTER VI

STOICS, EPICUREANS, AND NEO-PLATONISTS

The three great streams of thought flowing from the fount of ancient Greece and now irrigating the fertile mental fields of the twentieth century, are those to which we apply the terms, Stoicism, Epicureanism, and Neo-Platonism, respectively. Let us give to each of these a few moments' consideration.

STOICISM

The great school of the Stoics was founded at Athens, by Zeno, of Cyprus, who lived about 340-265 B. C. The Stoic philosophy was not original, but was quite eclectic in nature, many sources having been drawn upon by it, and additions made from time to time. Starting with the fundamental conception of Heraclitus—the idea of the Universal Spirit of Fire, ever changing and with mind as its essence—it absorbed much from Plato through Aristotle, adding much of the philosophy of the latter at the same time. The Stoic ideas changed from time to time, in minor particulars, but the general and fundamental conceptions remained much the same from first to last.

The Stoics were decidedly pantheistic. As Professor Tufts says: "The Stoics . . . developed the primitive animistic theory of the Cosmos in such a way as to make their conception capable of being characterized at once as pantheism and as materialism. This was effected through the conception of the Pneuma, which was, on the one hand, the all pervading and animating spirit or life of the universe, and, on the other, was still a material substance, a finer air or fiery breath. In this Pneuma each individual shares. Accordingly, to follow human nature means not only to follow human nature's highest principle of reason, but to conform to the all-pervading and controlling principle of the world, to the divine Law or Logos which characterizes the Pneuma in its rational aspect."

The "Pneuma" of the Stoics, and the other Greek thinkers, was not air or breath, as the name might indicate, but that subtle and transcendental principle which is often expressed as "Spirit." This active and universal principle—this Cosmic Spirit—was sometimes represented by the symbol of fire, owing to its incessant motion and changing manifestations. It was also represented by the general idea of "Spirit," without any attempt to define that term. This Spirit-Fire was held to be self-conscious—a great World-Soul, or *anima mundi.* It was the Absolute—Being—God. From it emanated or appeared earth and water, ether and air—the universe of shape, form and separate life. God was Nature—

and Nature, God. Nature was therefore rational. Life and mind were immanent and present everywhere. Every individual soul was but an expression, appearance or emanation of the great World-Soul. Every soul was individualized only temporarily, and would be eventually reabsorbed into the World-Soul, at the end of the cycle of manifestation—at the day of the triumph of the universal, all-devouring Fire. Each cycle of differentiation was destined to end, only to be succeeded by a new one—and so on to infinity.

This idea of the World-Soul was not new in Greek thought. The Stoics simply followed the rule of, "Take your own wherever you find it." Heraclitus and Anaxagoras had conceived the idea, and used it under their own terms. Plato used it, and, as Professor Tufts says, "attempted to embody in it the opposite principles of unity and plurality, of timeless being and changing process, which he usually contrasted so sharply. It was thus a mediating conception." In the centuries to follow, in European thought, the idea was adopted by Bruno (A. D. 1548-1600); Spinoza (1632-1677), and through the latter, in varying forms, by Herder, Lessing and Goethe. Schelling was largely under its influence; Hegel and Schopenhauer embodied it in their opposing conceptions, the lead of the latter being followed by von Hartmann; Herbert Spencer narrowly escapes it in his "Unknowable;" Emerson recognizes it in his

"Over-Soul;" modern Science assumes it partially in its Monism; and it is in evidence in "the present swing to pantheism" which has attracted the attention of the thinking world. The World-Spirit is the essence of pantheism. It is the conception of The All in All; and All in The All—God in nature, and nature in God.

Naturally arising from this fundamental conception, we find the Stoic philosophy of life in connection with which the school is now chiefly known. The Stoic creed was that of resignation—almost apathy. Fate or necessity ruled the universe through Unchanging Law. The soul of man, being divine, should not descend to allowing itself to be affected by the passions and things of sense, nor by the changing things of the objective world. The Stoic when told of some mighty impending calamity, said, "Well, what is that to me?" Self-control was esteemed the highest virtue. The passions were to be subordinated to reason and will. Mental disturbances, grief, worries, sorrow and pain, were but false judgments of mortal mind, and were to be overcome by true wisdom and a positive refusal to be subject to their sway. An authority says:

"The Stoic ethics was the ethics of apathy. The soul should not allow itself to be carried away by the passions aroused in it by external things. A man must be self-controlled. The passions are due to false judgments and mental disturbances, hence they can be overcome by wisdom, and by a refusal to assent to their dictation. A man is not, indeed, master of his fate, but he can keep his self-control and proud self-complacency through all the vicissitudes of life."

The Stoic ideal was a simple, natural life—for nature was divine, and to live near to her was to be more divine. Duty was derived from the Laws of Nature. The Stoics held that all men are brothers, because of their common origin and nature—all being manifestations of the one Spirit, or expressions of the one Over-Soul. This being so, it was held that it was their manifest duty to live in brotherly love and in a spirit of mutual helpfulness.

Distinctions of rank were held to be illusions and follies, and did not interfere with the social relations of the members of the school. Marcus Aurelius, the Roman Emperor, was a prominent Stoic, and wrote one of its classics; Epictetus, the slave, the author of the immortal "Discourses," was a Stoic. These two men, representing the two extremes of social rank, are perhaps the most widely known of the Stoics; this fact alone gives the Stoic idea and practice of the equality of spirit.

Prof. William James has said concerning the Stoic ideal:

"Neither threats nor pleadings can move a man unless they touch some one of his potential or actual selves. Only thus can we, as a rule, get a 'purchase' on another's will. The first care of diplomatists and monarchs and all who wish to rule or influence is, accordingly, to find out their victim's strongest principle of self-regard, so as to make that the fulcrum of all appeals. But if a man has given up those things which are subject to foreign fate, and ceased to regard them as parts of himself at all, we are well-nigh powerless over him. The Stoic recipe for contentment was *to dispossess yourself in advance of all that was out of your own power,*—then fortune's shocks might rain down unfelt. Epictetus exhorts us, by thus narrowing and at the same time solidifying ourself to make it invulnerable: 'I must die; well, but must I die groaning too? I will speak what appears to be right, and if the despot says, "Then I will put you to death," I will reply, "When did I ever tell you I was immortal? You will do your part, and I mine; it is yours to kill, and mine to die intrepid; yours to banish, mine to depart untroubled." How do we act in a voyage? We choose the pilot, the sailors, the hour. Afterwards comes a storm. What have I to care for? My part is performed. This matter belongs to the pilot. But the ship is sinking; what then have I to do? That which alone I can do—submit to be drowned without fear, without clamor or accusing of God, but as one who knows that what is born must likewise die.' This Stoic fashion, though efficacious and heroic enough in its place and time, is, it must be confessed, only possible as an habitual mood of the soul to narrow and unsympathetic characters. It proceeds altogether by exclusion. If I am a Stoic, the goods I cannot appropriate cease to be *my* goods, and the temptation lies very near to deny that they are goods at all. We find this mode of protecting the self by exclusion and denial very common among people who are in other respects not Stoics. All narrow people *intrench* their Me, they *retract* it,—from the region of what they cannot securely possess. People who don't resemble them, or who treat them with indifference, people over whom they gain no influence, are people on whose existence, however meritorious it may intrinsically be, they look with chill negation, if not with positive hate. Who will not be mine I will exclude from existence altogether; that is, as far as I can make it so, such people shall be as if they were not. Thus may a certain absoluteness and definiteness in the outline of my Me console me for the smallness of its content."

The concluding portions of the above quotation are interesting, when considered in the light of certain tendencies of modern philosophical thought. In spite of Prof. James's adverse comment, it is true that there is an increase of this spirit of the mental "shutting out" of unpleasant and unavoidable things and persons. In certain phases of the New Thought and similar movements we find the teaching of the "denial in consciousness" of undesirable circumstances and persons. Prof. James has stated but one side of the question—the latter-day Stoic insists upon the virtue of the opposite side.

Perhaps one of the most characteristic expressions of this latter-day Stoic spirit is found in that splendid poem of Henley, which has given courage and strength to so many in their hours of trial. I think it well to reproduce it at this point, in connection with this consideration of the spirit of the Stoic philosophy:

INVICTUS

BY W. E. HENLEY.

Out of the night that covers me,
Black as the pit from pole to pole,
I thank whatever gods there be
For my unconquerable soul.

In the fell clutch of circumstance
I have not winced or cried aloud;
Under the bludgeonings of chance
My head is bloody but unbowed.

Beyond this vale of doubt and fears
Looms but the terror of the Shade,
And yet the passing of the years
Finds, and shall find me, unafraid.

It matters not how straight the gate,
How charged with punishments the scroll;
I am the master of my fate,
I am the captain of my soul.

To those who have thought of Stoicism only in its phase of self-mastery and self-control, I would suggest a consideration of the beautiful devotional "Hymn to Zeus" by Cleanthes, who lived about 250 B. C. The legends relate that Cleanthes was a reformed pugilist, who for seventeen years attended the lectures of Zeno during the day, earning his livelihood by manual labor at night. He afterward succeeded to the leadership of the school. His celebrated hymn is regarded as a classic. The following is according to the translation of Dr. James Adams:

CLEANTHES' "HYMN TO ZEUS."

O God most glorious, called by many a name,
Nature's great king, through endless years the same;
Omnipotence, who by thy just decree
Controllest all, hail, Zeus, for unto thee
Behoves thy creatures in all lands to call.
We are thy children, we alone of all
On earth's broad ways that wander to and fro,
Bearing thine image wheresoe'er we go.
Wherefore with songs of praise thy power I will forth show.
Lo! yonder heaven, that round the earth is wheeled,
Follows thy guidance, still to thee doth yield
Glad homage; thine unconquerable hand
Such flaming minister, the levin-brand,
Wieldeth, a sword two-edged, whose deathless might
Pulsates through all that Nature brings to light;
Vehicle of the universal Word, that flows
Through all, and in the light celestial glows

Of stars both great and small. O King of Kings
Through ceaseless ages, God, whose purpose brings
To birth, whate'er on land or in the sea
Is wrought, or in high heaven's immensity;
Save what the sinner works infatuate.
Nay, but thou knowest to make crooked straight:
Chaos to thee is order: in thine eyes
The unloved is lovely, who did'st harmonize
Things evil with things good, that there should be
One Word through all things everlastingly.
One Word—whose voice alas! the wicked spurn;
Insatiate for the good their spirits yearn:
Yet seeing see not, neither hearing hear
God's universal law, which those revere,
By reason guided, happiness who win.
The rest, unreasoning, diverse shapes of sin
Self-prompted follow: for an idle name
Vainly they wrestle in the lists of fame:
Others inordinately Riches woo,
Or dissolute, the joys of flesh pursue.
Now here, now there they wander, fruitless still,
For ever seeking good and finding ill.
Zeus the all-bountiful, whom darkness shrouds,
Whose lightning lightens in the thunder clouds;
Thy children save from error's deadly sway:
Turn thou the darkness from their souls away:
Vouchsafe that unto knowledge they attain;
For thou by knowledge art made strong to reign
O'er all, and all things rulest righteously.
So by the honored, we will honor thee,
Praising thy works continually with songs,
As mortals should; nor higher meed belongs
E'en to the gods, that justly do adore
The universal Law for evermore.

To many good orthodox folk this beautiful hymn, coming from such a decidedly "heathen" source, will be a revelation of the fact that the spirit of worship does not belong to any particular age or especial creed, and that, as the ancient Hindu sage has said: "The Truth is one—though men call it by many names."

EPICUREANISM

The great school of the Epicureans was founded in Athens, about 300 B. C., by Epicurus, a celebrated philosopher of Samos, of whom an authority says:

"He taught that the true end of existence is a species of quietism, in which the philosopher holds himself open to all the pleasurable sensations which the temperate indulgence of his ordinary appetites, and the recollection of past, with the anticipation of future enjoyments, are sufficiently abundant to supply. . . . Owing to a misrepresentation, he is generally held to have taught gross sensualism, and his name is applied to the idea of sensual enjoyments, particularly those of the table."

Another authority says:

"The system of Epicurus and his tenets and teach'ngs have been the subjects of gross misrepresentation and dense misunderstanding. To the popular mind the system has become the archetype of gross sensualism. In truth, Epicurus' cardinal doctrine was that the chief end of man was to be happy. And in the pursuit of that happiness all means of pleasure or enjoyment were to be allowed. Thus, if it gave pleasure to an ascetic to starve himself and to scourge his flesh, it was as much allowable for him to pursue these methods of attaining happiness, pleasure, or peace of mind, as was the eating or drinking of the voluptuary. No matter what the choice of instruments, the end to be attained was pleasure. If one man found pleasure in books, he was as much an Epicurean, if he sought his favorite enjoyment, as was the sleek, lazy Sybarite, who passed his existence in pandering his grosser nature. Epicureanism may be briefly defined as a supreme effort at enjoyment."

Epicurus taught a philosophy which was, in the end, rather a method of life than a search for ultimate truth—a moral philosophy, rather than a natural philosophy or a metaphysic. He, however, laid a basis of natural philosophy upon which to erect his philosophy of living. He favored Democritus' theory of a material universe composed of atoms, the play, action and reaction, of the latter accounting for the phenomenal world. His idea came very close to that of the materialists of the nineteenth century. He believed in the gods of the Greeks, but held that they dwelt apart and separate from man, having no concern with or interest in the universe of men and things, and were therefore not to be feared. In fact, he held that the great evil of life was fear, particularly the fear of the gods and of death. The fear of the gods he disposes of as above stated; the fear of death he brushed away by the teaching that death is nothing, *for when we are living and knowing, death is not; and when death is, we are not living and knowing;* and, likewise: "Where *we* are, *death* is not—where *death* is, *we* are not." He said: "Good and evil are only where they are felt, and death is the absence of all feeling." He held that health of body, accompanied by tranquillity of mind, represent the requisites for happiness. Pleasure, he held, is the first and great good, but he recognized pain as necessary as a background and revealer of pleasure. He also taught that many forms of pleasure were to be avoided, as they brought greater pain in their train. There was even a trace of the opposing Stoic philosophy in certain of his teachings regarding happiness and pleasure, for he said: "If thou wilt make a man happy, add not to his riches, but rather take away from his desires." He also held that the greatest happiness and pleasure arise from a compliance with virtue and honor, saying: "We cannot live a life of pleasure which is not also a life of prudence, honor, and justice; nor lead a life of prudence, honor and justice which is not also a life of pleasure."

It is one of the ironies of history that Epicurus, the teacher of a system of happiness and pleasure based upon reason, prudence, justice, honor and virtue, should come to be popularly known as the teacher of gross sensualism and base gratification of the appetites. Nevertheless, to philosophers and students of philosophy, he is known for what he was and what he taught. His life and conduct were exemplary, and his influence operated for good. Many points of his teaching have survived, and have exerted a marked influence upon the thought of later days.

NEO-PLATONISM

Another great channel of the Platonic ideas, and one which has had a most marked influence upon the thought of the succeeding centuries, culminating in the modern revival of the old ideals of past thinkers, is that of the Neo-Platonic school. *Neo-Platonism is the direct channel through which the thought of Plato reached Emerson and the Transcendentalists.* The latter school and its great exponent freely acknowledge their indebtedness, and the connection becomes quite apparent when the two teachings are compared. Modern idealism and the inclination toward mysticism owe a similar debt, for the connection is direct and uninterrupted throughout the centuries. Neo-Platonism is the great connecting link between the transcendental philosophy of ancient Greece and that of modern Europe and America. Neo-Platonism is defined by Dewey as: "The revival and transformation of Platonic philosophy that took place, with Alexandria as its headquarters, under the influence of Oriental thought." Here the headquarters of the Oriental and the Grecian thought met and mingled, and formed a new philosophical stream which was destined to carry the barque of thought down through the centuries, into lands then unknown and undreamed of. It will be well worth our time to acquaint ourself with its history.

Neo-Platonism had its original home in Alexandria, and was a phase of the Alexandrian School of philosophical thought. Professor Wenley says of the Alexandrian School:

"It indicates that junction between Eastern and Western thought which took place at Alexandria and produced a new series of doctrines which mark an entire school. Although these tendencies may be traced as far back as 280 B. C. . . . it is convenient to date the *floreat* of the school from 30 B. C. to 529 A. D. . . . The beginnings of the movement are almost lost in obscurity. Some profess to find traces of it so early as the Ceptuagint (280 B. C.), but it is usual to date the first overt traces from Aristobolus (160 B. C.). The Jewish line culminated in Philo (40 A. D.), who accepted Greek metaphysical ideas, and by the aid of allegorical interpretation found their justification in the Hebrew Scriptures. . . . East and West met and commingled at Alexandria. The operative ideas of the civilizations, cultures and religions of Rome, Greece, Palestine, and the further East found themselves in juxtaposition. Hence arose a new problem, developed partly by Occidental thought, partly by Oriental aspiration. Religion and philosophy became inextricably mixed, and the resultant doctrines consequently belong to neither sphere proper, but are rather witnesses to an attempt at combining both."

Neo-Platonism was the expression of the philosophical side of the Alexandrian School. Lewes says that "their originality consisted in having employed the Platonic Dialectics as a guide to Mysticism and Pantheism; in having connected the doctrine of the East with the dialectics of the Greeks; in having made reason the justification of faith. By their dialectics they were Platonists; by their theory of the trinity they were Mystics; by their principle of emanation they were pantheists." Wenley says: "Philosophically viewed, the school is eminently eclectic. Although relying upon Plato for its first principles, and especially for its dualism, it agrees with the post-Aristotelian skeptics in its contempt for knowledge; with the Stoics in its manifold tendencies toward pantheism, and in its regard for an ascetic morality; it bears traces, too, of the influence of Aristotle, especially in some aspects of its statement of the problem of the relation of God to the world."

Speaking generally, it may be said that the Neo-Platonists held that the basis of nature was "The One," an abstract principle of Unity. From this Unity, the source of all things, emanated the principle of Pure Intelligence. From the latter emanated the World-Soul, or *anima mundi*. The World-Soul then manifested in the individual souls of men and animals. The later Neo-Platonists went very far in asserting the Divine Immanence in the World-Soul, and consequently in the individual souls, and their conception was really that of a pantheistic idealism. Ammonius Saccas (A. D. 200) may be said to have been the father of Neo-Platonism in its aspect of mysticism. He devoted great attention to the soul, explaining its nature, fall, and destiny, including the possibility and means of its returning to the state of transcendental bliss from which it originally fell. The real home of the soul, he held, was on the transcendental plane, and its only hope of happiness was to be found in a return to that plane. To be saved, the soul must rise above the world of experience and enter into the higher realm of thought and life.

These mystics held (as have all other mystics, regardless of country or age) that the individual soul might rise above the world of sense experience, and enter into an ecstatic condition, in which they were transported to the transcendental plane. Some called this state of ecstasy, and its result, as "the Union with God." Pringle-Pattison says of this feature of mystic practice: "Penetrated by the thought of the ultimate unity of all existence, and impatient of even a seeming separation from the creative source of things, mysticism succumbs to a species of metaphysical fascination. Its ideal becomes that of passive contemplation, in which the distinctions of individuality disappear, and the finite spirit achieves, as it were, utter union or identity with the Being of things. As this goal cannot be reached under the conditions of relation and distinction which ordinary human thought imposes, mysticism asserts the existence of a supra-rational experience in which this union is realized. Such is the intuition or ecstasy or mystical swoon of the Eastern mystics, the mystical or metaphysical 'love' of the Neo-Platonists, and the 'gifts' of the medieval saints." The same authority says: "In its attempt to transcend the bounds of reason and to exalt the divine above all anthropomorphic predicates, mysticism leaves us, as in Neo-Platonism, with the empty abstraction of the nameless and supra-essential One —the One which transcends both knowledge and existence."

It is interesting to note in this connection that the revival of the ideas of Neo-Platonism in modern thought has brought about a tendency on the part of certain schools of modern mystic metaphysics to revive the mystic swoon, visions and transcendental ecstasies of the older school. The frequent modern use of the term "cosmic consciousness" in this connection, and the numerous modern recitals of experiences of this kind, show an astonishing correspondence to the "Union with God" and "Ecstasy," of the Neo-Platonist mystics. (It may be of some interest to note at this point that the Stoics had used the term "Cosmos" as one form of expression of the World-Soul or *anima mundi.*) The mysticism so noticeable in certain schools of modern popular metaphysics shows plainly its direct descent from Neo-Platonism, usually through Emerson and the Transcendental Movement.

Plotinus (A. D. 240) was one of the most brilliant of the Neo-Platonists. He was a Greek Theosophist and Mystic, and added to the popularity of the mystic Union with God, and similar transcendental beliefs and practices. Porphyry, Iamblichus, Sopater, Maximus, Plutarch and Proclus were prominent in the school, and gave to it a decided movement away from its former philosophic aspect, and toward its mystical, occult and fantastic semi-religious aspect. Coming in contact with the rising tide of Early Christianity, the movement gradually weakened, but, nevertheless, before dying out it managed to impress itself strongly upon the new religion.

Many of the early fathers of the Church were strongly impressed by the Neo-Platonic influence, and their writings read strangely in the light of the later theology of the Church, although closely akin to the still later writings of the mystics of the last few centuries of European thought. Clement of Alexandria, and Origen, early fathers of the Church, were strongly impressed with Neo-Platonism. The sect of Gnostics, which arose in the early Christian Church in the second and third centuries of the Christian era, were largely influenced by the Neo-Platonic teachings, especially regarding the relation of the universe to God, in which they held to the theory of "emanation." Students of the early history of the Christian Church are constantly confronted with the influence of Neo-Platonism, and many writers have traced the effect of the same upon the Church doctrines of to-day. Finally driven from Alexandria and Rome, Neo-Platonism took refuge in Athens, its original source, and was finally suppressed by Justinian in 529 A. D.

But though supposedly dead and safely buried, the spirit of Neo-Platonism persisted in appearing to its friends. In the fifteenth century a remarkable revival of the old teachings took place. Nicolas of Cusa and other mystics found life in the old flame when the breath of interest was applied to its smoldering embers. Nicolas taught the doctrine of the possibility of divine knowledge through ecstatic states and transcendental "intuition." Others, at different intervals, would bring the attention of the world to the almost forgotten doctrines.

Finally in the seventeenth century there occurred that remarkable revival of Neo-Platonism in England, under the influence of Cudworth and Henry More, the followers of whom became known as "the Cambridge Platonists," the movement being centered chiefly at the University of Cambridge. The Cambridge Platonists were principally clergymen and scholars who had become dissatisfied with the trend of theological and philosophical thought of their day. Showing a strong tendency toward mysticism, idealism and a modified pantheism, they soon formed an important school of thought of their time. Plato, the Neo-Platonists, especially Plotinus, Descartes, Mallebranche and Boehme, the mystic philosopher, were their principal sources of thought and inspiration. Cudworth postulated the existence of a plastic nature which was akin to the Demiurge or World-Soul of the Greeks, although he held that it was a working instrument and aid to God, rather than God himself. More presented a subtle and fascinating doctrine of mysticism. The movement attracted many men of note and distinction, both to its inner circle and to its affiliated schools of general sympathizers. Traces of its influence still exist in English literature and philosophy.

It may interest the reader to have presented to him the idea of plastic nature, as advanced by

Ralph Cudworth (A. D. 1617-88), the English Neo-Platonist, particularly as the detailed teaching is seldom met with in works upon the subject. Cudworth says:

"It seems not so agreeable to reason that Nature, as a distinct thing from the Deity, should be quite superseded or made to signify nothing, God, Himself, doing all things immediately and miraculously; from whence it would follow also that they are all done either forcibly and violently, or else artificially only, and none of them by any inward principle of their own. This opinion is further confuted by that slow and gradual process that in the generation of things, which would seem to be but a vain and idle pomp or a trifling formality if the moving power were omnipotent; as also by those errors and bungles which are committed where the matter is inept and contumacious; which argue that the moving power be not irresistible, and that Nature is such a thing as is not altogether incapable (as well as human art) of being sometimes frustrated and disappointed by the indisposition of matter. Whereas an omnipotent moving power, as it could dispatch its work in a moment, so would it always do it infallibly and irresistibly, no ineptitude and stubbornness of matter being ever able to hinder such a one, or make him bungle or fumble in anything. Wherefore, since neither all things are produced fortuitously, or by the unguided mechanism of matter, nor God himself may be reasonably thought to do all things immediately and miraculously, it may well be concluded that there is a Plastic Nature under him, which, as an inferior and subordinate instrument, doth drudgingly execute that part of the providence which consists in the regular and orderly motion of matter; yet so as there is also besides this a higher providence to be acknowledged, which, presiding over it, doth often supply the defects in it, and sometimes overrules it, forasmuch as the Plastic Nature cannot act electively nor with discretion."

The reader will recognize in this conception of "Plastic Nature" a successor of the "Universal Flame" of Heraclitus, and the "Will-to-Live" of the

Buddhists, as well as a predecessor of the "Will" of Schopenhauer, von Hartmann, and Nietzche, and the "Life-Forces" of Bernard Shaw—with this difference, that in these conceptions nature and God are identified, instead of being considered as co-existent. Cudworth anticipated Schopenhauer's objection that when one identifies God with nature he really "shows God to the door"—for a self-existent nature is a no less-thinkable proposition than a self-existent God manifesting as nature. Cudworth's conception is interesting not only by reason of its quaint presentation, but also as a notable attempt to bridge the chasm between theism and pantheism. It deserves greater recognition than is generally accorded it by modern writers on the history of philosophy.

CHAPTER VII

THE ORIENTAL FOUNT

The student of the changing conceptions of modern Western thought is keenly aware of the remarkable influence being exerted by the centuries-old philosophies and metaphysics of India and other countries of the Orient. This is all the more remarkable when it is remembered that until about fifty or sixty years ago it was practically impossible to obtain an English translation of the leading Hindu philosophical works. And other countries were but little better off, as we may see when we consider that Schopenhauer, when he wished to study the *Upanishads,* was unable to find the principal books translated into English or German, and was compelled to gather up fragments translated in several languages, and then to have them retranslated into German. But the work of Max Muller and other Orientalists have now placed in our hands careful translations of the Sacred Books of the East, and the result is that the subtle essence of the Oriental thought has permeated every circle of philosophical, metaphysical and religious thought. The influence of the Theosophical Society has done much in the direction of familiarizing the Western world with certain of the Oriental ideas, and the World's Fair Parliament of Religions did much to call the attention of the West to the buried riches of the Eastern thought.

The student who begins the task of penetrating into the maze of Hindu thought is at once struck with the remarkable resemblance of the ideas enunciated thousands of years ago in India to the much later ideas of ancient Greece, and the two thousand years still later conception of modern Western thinkers. There is an unbroken thread of thought running through them all, upon which the various philosophical and metaphysical systems have been strung like beads. Edward Carpenter has well said:

"We seem to be arriving at a time when, with the circling of our knowledge of the globe, a great synthesis of all human thought on the ancient and ever-engrossing problem of Creation is quite naturally and inevitably taking shape. The world-old wisdom of the Upanishads, with their profound and impregnable doctrine of the Universal Self, the teachings of Buddha or of Lao-Tze, the poetic insight of Plato, the inspired sayings of Jesus and Paul, the speculations of Plotinus, or of the Gnostics, and the wonderful contributions of later European thought, from the fourteenth century mystics down through Spinoza, Berkeley, Kant, Hegel, Schopenhauer, Ferrier and others; all these, combining with the immense mass of material furnished by modern physical and biological science, and psychology, are preparing a great birth, as it were; and out of this meeting of elements is already arising a dim outline of a philosophy which must surely dominate human thought for a long period. A new philosophy we can hardly expect, or wish for; since indeed *the same germinal thoughts of the Vedic authors come all the way down history*, even to Schopenhauer and Whitman, inspiring philosophy after philosophy and religion after religion."

Having its head-waters back in the early centuries

of history, the Hindu philosophical thought has flowed down through the ages, irrigating and nourishing many fertile fields of philosophy, metaphysics and religion. There is very little, if anything, in these fields of thought which may not be traced back to the Hindu influence. Max Muller and Paul Duessen have borne evidence that in the Vedas and the Upanishads may be found the seed-thoughts for every philosophical conception that the Western mind has ever evolved. As an authority has said: "Every possible form of human philosophical speculation, conception or theory has been advanced by some Hindu philosopher during the centuries. It would seem that the Hindu philosophical mind has acted as the finest sieve, through which strained the volume of human philosophical thought, every idea of importance being gathered and applied, by someone, at some time, in India."

Victor Cousins said: "When we read the poetical and philosophical monuments of the far East—above all those of India, which are beginning to spread in Europe, we discover there many a truth, and truths so profound, and which make such a contrast with the meanness of the results at which European genius has sometimes stopped, that we are constrained to bend the knee before the philosophy of the East, and to see in this cradle of the human race the native land of the highest philosophy. . . . India contains the whole history of philosophy in a nutshell."

Sir Monier Williams says: "Indeed, if I may be allowed the anachronism, the Hindus were Spinozites more than two thousand years before the existence of Spinoza; and Darwinians many centuries before Darwin; and Evolutionists many centuries before the doctrine of Evolution had been accepted by the scientists of our time, and before any word like 'Evolution' existed in any language of the world."

Prof. Hopkins says: "Plato was full of Sankhyan thought, worked out by him, but taken from Pythagoras. Before the sixth century, B. C., all the religio-philosophical ideas of Pythagoras were current in India. If there were but one or two of these cases they might be set aside as accidental coincidences, but such coincidences are too numerous to be the result of chance." Davies says: "Kapila's system is the first formulated system of philosophy of which the world has a record. It is the earliest attempt on record to give an answer, from reason alone, to the mysterious questions which arise in every thoughtful mind about the origin of the world, the nature and relations of man and his future destiny. . . . The human intellect has gone over the same ground that it occupied more than two thousand years ago." Hopkins says: "Both Thales and Parmenides were indeed anticipated by Hindu sages, and the Eleatic school seems but a reflection of the Upanishads." Schlegel says: "Even the loftiest philosophy of the Europeans, the idealism of reason as it is set forth by the Greek philosophers, appears in comparison with the abundant light and vigor of Oriental idealism like a feeble Promethean spark in the full flood of heavenly glory of the noonday sun, faltering and feeble and ever ready to be extinguished."

The Orient—India in particular—is the home of the Idealistic Philosophy which is now exerting such an influence on Western thought. So closely identified with idealism is the highest Hindu philosophy that to the average person all Hindu philosophy is identified with idealism. But this is quite wrong. India, the home of idealism, and whose thought has carried that doctrine to its last refinement of tenuity, is also the home of every other form of philosophical thought which has ever been evolved from the mind of man. As far back as the time of Buddha, we find there had been in existence for many centuries various schools of philosophical thought far removed from idealism, many of which have been revamped or rediscovered by modern Western thinkers. We find some of the oldest Buddhistic writings vigorously combating these heterodox schools and pointing to their errors. The following quotation from Dr. J. E. Carpenter will surprise many readers: He says:

"The eagerness with which the speculations concerning the 'self' were pursued may be inferred from the conspectus of sixty wrong views about it, according to the Buddha. . . . On the other hand, there were teachers daring enough to deny the first principles on which the Brahmanical were all based, viz., *karma*.

Such among the Buddha's contemporaries were the agnostic Sanjaya, who repudiated all knowledge of the subject; the materialist Ajita of the hairy garment, who allowed no other life, rejected the claim to knowledge by higher insight, and resolved man into the four elements—earth, water, fire, air—which dispersed at death; the indifferentist Purana Kassapa, who acknowledged no moral distinctions, and consequently no merit or reward; and the determinist Makkhali of the Cow-pen, who indeed recognized the *samsara* (the chain of rebirth and phenomenal existence), but admitted no voluntary action, and hence no *karma* (the fruit of action), each individual only working out the law of its nature which it could not modify or control, the sole cause of everything being found in *niyati*, destiny, impersonal necessity, or fate."

In addition to the schools mentioned above, the Hindu school of materialism, the Charvakas, or Lokayatikas, was founded about three thousand years ago, and has always had a following, although despised by the orthodox Hindus. The Charvakas not only held to the material nature of the universe and all things contained therein, but also held that the individual perished at the death of the body, there being no such thing as a soul. They held to the ideal: "Eat, drink and be merry, for to-morrow we die." They denounced the priests as impostors, and all religions as fallacies designed to delude and rob the people, and reviled the Vedas, or Sacred Books, as drivel and falsehood cleverly formulated to delude and control the people. These doctrines will have a familiar sound to the Western reader of to-day—and yet they were current in India from five hundred to one thousand years before the Christian era, and have had followers ever since.

In philosophy, and in religion, India has given birth to the highest possible and lowest possible conceptions. There have been no heights to which the Hindu mind has feared to climb, and there have been no depths into which it has not descended. The most refined ideals and the most gross conceptions have been entertained by the Hindus. The mental and spiritual soil which has given nourishment to the noblest philosophical plants and trees, from which have come the fairest flowers and the richest fruits, has also given life to the most noxious weeds and the most poisonous varieties of mental and spiritual fungi. In the garden of Oriental thought, one searching for the rarest and most beautiful flowers and richest fruit will find it—but he must beware of the mental toad-stools, spiritual deadly night-shade, and psychic loco-weed which beset the paths. In Hindu thought the extremes meet—it is the land of the spiritual paradox.

While it is true that the various orthodox Hindu schools of philosophical thought apparently differ materially from each other, it will be found that these differences are but upon points of interpretation and theories of the manner in which the One reality manifests as the Many of the phenomenal world. In other words, the differences are regarding the "*how*" of the manifestation, rather than the fundamental principles themselves. Under the various schools of the Hindu thought will be found a common fundamental principle of the One Life and One Self of the universe. All true Hindu thought believes that the ultimate Reality is One, and that the phenomenal universe is composed of manifold and varied manifestations, emanations, or reflections of that One. It is the same fundamental thought that caused the Grecian conception of the World-Spirit. Whether this One be called the Absolute, Brahman, Krishna, or simply "That," by the various Hindu schools, it is always regarded as One.

The Hindu philosophy is essentially monistic. It holds that All is One, and One is All—that the One is all that is, ever has been, ever will be, or ever can be. Beyond the One there is held to be but Nothing—illusion, *maya*, "mortal mind." It is more than monistic—it is *ultra*-monistic.

Swami Vivekananda, the apostle of the Vedanta Philosophy of India, who visited this country several years ago, attracting marked attention from many of the best minds of our land, brings out this fundamental idea of the Hindu philosophy in the following extracts from his lectures. He said:

"Where is there any more misery for him who sees this Oneness in the universe, this Oneness of life, Oneness of everything? . . . This separation between man and man, man and woman, man and child, nation from nation, earth from moon, moon from sun, this separation between atom and atom is the cause really of all the misery, and the Vedanta says this separation does not exist, it is not real. It is merely apparent, on the surface. In the heart of things there is unity still. If you go inside you will find that unity between man and man, women and children, races and races, high and low, rich and poor, the gods and men; all are One, and animals, too, if you go deep enough, and he who has attained to that has no more delusion. Where is there any more delusion for him? What can delude him? He knows the reality of everything, the secret of everything. Where is there any more misery for him? What does he desire? He has traced the reality of everything unto the Lord, that center, that Unity of everything, and that is Eternal Bliss, Eternal Knowledge, Eternal Existence. Neither death nor disease nor sorrow nor discontent is there. . . . In the Center, the reality, there is no one to be mourned for, no one to be sorry for. He has penetrated everything, the Pure One, the Formless, the Bodyless, the Stainless. He is the Knower, He is the great Poet, the Self-Existent. He who is giving to everyone what he deserves. . . . When man has seen himself as One with the infinite Being of the universe, when all separateness has ceased, when all men, all women, all angels, all gods, all animals, all plants, the whole universe has been melted into that oneness, then all fear disappears. Whom to fear? Can I hurt myself? Can I kill myself? Can I injure myself? Do you fear yourself? Then will all sorrow disappear. What can cause me sorrow? I am the One Existence of the universe. Then all jealousies will disappear; of whom to be jealous? Of myself? Then all bad feelings disappear. Against whom shall I have this bad feeling? Against myself? There is none in the universe but me . . . kill out this differentiation, kill out this superstition that there are many. 'He who, in this world of many, sees that One; he who, in this mass of insentiency, sees that One Sentient Being; he who in this world of shadow catches that Reality, unto him belongs eternal peace, unto none else, unto none else.'"

We find in the above expression of Hindu Monism the keynote that is predominant in the modern Western philosophical, metaphysical and theological thought. All that modern Western Monistic Idealism is asserting so strongly has been asserted, centuries before, and even more strongly, by the Hindu sages. Compare the above utterances of the world-old truths of the Vedanta, as voiced by Vivekananda, with the latter-day utterances. In the Christian Science text-book, "Science and Health," by Mary Baker G. Eddy, on the page preceding the table of contents, we find several quotations, one of which is as follows:

> "I, I, I, I, itself, I,
> The inside and outside, the what and the why,
> The when and the where, the low and the high,
> All I, I, I, I, itself, I."

In the same book we find the following given as "The Scientific Statement of Being":

> "There is no life, truth, intelligence nor substance in matter. All is infinite Mind and its infinite manifestation, for God is All in all. Spirit is immortal Truth; matter is mortal error. Spirit is the real and eternal; matter is the unreal and temporal. Spirit is God, and man is His image and likeness; hence man is spiritual and not material."

Emerson says of the "OverSoul":

> "Truth, goodness and beauty are but different faces of the same All. . . . God is, and all things are but shadows of him. . . . The True doctrine of omnipresence is that God reappears with all His parts in every moss and cobweb. The value of the universal contrives to throw itself into every point."

Do not these ideas breathe the very spirit of the inner Hindu thought?

This idea of the Immanent God, or the Higher Pantheism, is permeating the thought of to-day, as we have shown in our first paper of the series. In that paper we quoted the following from the articles of Harold Bolce, in the *Cosmopolitan Magazine*:

"Not only in religious rhetoric, but in reality, the school men say, is man the avatar of God. . . . They say that . . . this is not an atheistic banishment of God and his holy angels, but is, on the contrary, the enthronement of a new Jehovah—a God that has become conscious and potent in the human mind."

Among some of the "New Thought" cults we hear of teachers boldly asserting and teaching their pupils to assert, that:

"I am God! There is None other than God! Therefore, as I AM, I must be God! Otherwise, I *am not* at all."

One of the widely printed bits of "advanced thought" verse is the following, which brings out very plainly the essence of the higher pantheism in modern thought:

"Thou great, eternal infinite, the great unbounded Whole,
Thy body is the universe—thy spirit is the soul.
If thou dost fill immensity; if thou art all in all;
If thou wert here before I was, I am not here at all.
How could I live outside of thee? Dost thou fill earth and air?
There surely is no place for me, outside of everywhere.
If thou art God, and thou dost fill immensity of space,
Then I am God, think as you will, or else I have no place.
And if I have no place at all, or if I am not here,
'Banished' I surely cannot be, for then I'd be somewhere.
Then I must be a part of God, no matter if I'm small;
And if I'm not a part of him, there's no such God at all."

Is not the spirit of the Hindu thought manifested throughout this Western expression? Prof. William James says:

"We may fairly suppose that the authority which absolute monism undoubtedly possesses, and probably always will possess over some persons, draws its strength far less from the intellectual than from mystical grounds. To interpret absolute monism worthily, be a mystic. . . . Observe how radical the theory of the monism here is. Separation is not simply overcome by the One, it is denied to exist. There is no many. We are not parts of the One; it has no parts, and since in a sense we undeniably *are*, it must be that each of us *is* the One, indivisibly and totally. *An Absolute One, and I that One*, surely we have here a religion which, emotionally considered, has a high pragmatic value; it imparts a perfect sumptuosity of security."

CHAPTER VIII

VEDANTISM, BUDDHISM, ZOROASTRIANISM AND SUFIISM

While there are many great schools, and still more minor-schools, of Oriental religio-philosophical thought, still our purpose may be realized by a brief consideration of the four great schools of the thought of the Orient which have had the greatest influence upon modern Western thought and speculation. These schools are, respectively, (1) Vedantism, that great philosophic school of India, the conceptions of which transcend even the most daring speculations of the Western philosophers; (2) Buddhism, that great school which has now almost passed away from India, its birthplace, but which has many millions of followers in China, Japan, and other countries, and whose influence has had a very marked effect upon Western thought; (3) Zoroastrianism, that once famous school of Persia, which has now almost entirely passed from the scene, but which has exerted a great influence upon schools of thought of other countries and later times; and (4) Sufiism, that strange mystical inner-teaching of the Mohammedan religion, upon which it was grafted by some ancient teachers in order to protect it from destruction by the new religion of Islam. Let us take a brief glance at each of these four important schools of thought.

VEDANTISM

The Vedanta school of philosophy is generally held to represent the highest flight of the Oriental philosophical thought. It dates far back in the centuries of the past, the best authorities generally holding that it was founded about 700 B. C., although even then probably founded upon older teachings. It embraces many minor schools under its general class, being in fact one of the most catholic of the philosophies. As Max Muller says: "The Vedanta philosophy leaves to every man a wide sphere of real usefulness, and places him under a law as strict and as binding as anything can be in this transitory life; it leaves him a Deity to worship as omnipotent and majestic as the deities of any other religion. It has room for almost every religion; nay, it embraces them all. Other Oriental philosophies do exist and have some following, but Vedanta has the largest."

The Vedanta philosophy is the extreme of absolute idealism. By "absolute idealism" is meant the philosophical conception that denies the existence of the phenomenal world apart from the universal mind. Absolute idealism denies the existence of material objects, holding that their appearances are merely ideas of the universal mind. In the Vedanta, the highest phase of Hindu philosophical thought, the teaching is that the Absolute, Brahman, or the Divine Mind is "an absolutely homogeneous, pure intelligence or thought, eternal, infinite, changeless, indivisible." This being the case, it becomes necessary for the Vedantin to account for "the appearance of the phenomenal world, with its succession of change, and its plurality of souls." But the Vedantin does not shrink from the responsibility, but faces it boldly. He accounts for the world of phenomena upon the theory of *maya* (illusion) arising from *avidya* (ignorance). But this ignorance and illusion is held to be universal, and not confined to individuals. The individual is bound by it until the scales fall from his eyes, and he sees the truth of the Oneness. An ancient Vedanta teacher, living many centuries ago, said: "The entire complex of phenomenal existence is considered as true so long as the Brahman and the Self has not arisen, just as the phantoms of a dream are considered to be dreams until the sleeper wakes." Thus the existence of the phenomenal world, while apparently real, is but the fiction of an illusory dream. It seemingly exists, while the state of ignorance persists, for, as Tennyson says: "Dreams are true, *while they last.*"

Max Muller has said:

"Vedanta holds a most unique position among the philosophies of the world. After lifting the Self or the true nature of the Ego, Vedanta unites it with the essence of Divinity, which is absolutely pure, perfect, immortal, unchangeable, and one. No philosopher, not even Plato, Spinoza, Kant, Hegel, or Schopenhauer has reached that height of philosophical thought. . . . None of our philosophers, not excepting Heraclitus, Plato, Kant or Hegel, has ventured to erect such a spire, never frightened by storms of lightnings. Stone follows upon stone, in regular succession after once the first step has been made, after once it has been seen that in the beginning there can have been but One, as there will be but One in the end, whether we call it Atman or Brahman."

Arising from this extreme theory of absolute idealism, we may see the various modern doctrines of idealism, from Berkeley to the modern schools of New Thought. The basic principle is that "All is Mind," and that all the phenomenal universe must exist as ideas, dreams, or pictures in that mind.

Edward Carpenter says:

"We see that there is in man a creative thought-source continually in operation, which is shaping and giving form not only to his body, but largely to the world in which he lives. In fact, the houses, the gardens, the streets among which we live, the clothes we wear, the books we read, have been produced from this source. And there is not one of these things—the building in which we are at this moment, the conveyance in which we may ride home—*which has not in its first birth* been a mere phantom thought in some man's mind, and owes its existence to that fact. Some of us who live in the midst of what we call civilization simply live embedded among the thoughts of other people. We see, hear, and touch those thoughts, and they are, for us, the World. But no sooner do we arrive at this point, and see the position clearly, than another question inevitably rises upon us. If, namely, this world of civilized life, with its great buildings and bridges and wonderful works of art, is the embodiment and materialization of the *thoughts of Man*, how about that other world of the mountains and the trees and the mighty ocean and the sunset sky—the world of Nature—is that also the embodiment and materialization of *the thoughts of other beings, or of one other Being?* And when we touch these things are we also coming into touch with the thoughts of these beings?"

The Vedanta is then seen to be based upon the fundamental thought that there exists but One Reality, and that, consequently, all else that seems to exist is but *maya* or illusion. This One reality is called "Brahman" or "That," the latter term being applied by some of its philosophers who hold that no *name* should be applied to the Nameless One. Brahman is held to be "beyond qualities or attributes; beyond subject or object; the efficient cause of the universe in its mental and material appearance; creator and created; doer and deed; cause and effect; self-existent; absolute; infinite; eternal; indivisible and immutable; all that is, ever has been, or ever will be." Max Muller states the Vedanta philosophy in a nutshell when he says: *"In one-half verse I shall tell you what has been taught in thousands of volumes: Brahman is true, the world is false; the soul is Brahman and nothing else."*

The Vedantist holds that there being but One, and that one being Brahman, there can be nothing else than Brahman; hence, the phenomenal universe, including the idea of individual souls, is mere *maya* or illusion; the universe being *but an idea in the mind of Brahman*—a mere reverie, meditation, or day-dream of the Absolute One. This then is the essence of the Vedanta, the remainder of the teachings being but an attempt to work out the how of the manifestation of the illusory universe which arises from "Maya, the inexplicable illusion, self-imagined. that is illusorily overspread upon Brahman." It is taught that "the total period of the creation, existence, and death of the universe is but as the twinkle of an eye to Brahm."

The position of Christian Science is that the Divine Mind images and idealizes *only the things and qualities which, like itself, are pure and perfect;* and that therefore all that is not pure and perfect cannot be the idea of the Divine Mind, but must, on the contrary, be the product of "mortal mind" and, therefore, must be unreal, untrue, illusion, error, lies. This position is also taken by many of the independent metaphysical cults of the day, who have come under the influence of the Christian Science teachings, and who have appropriated some of its fundamental ideas. But differ as may the modern schools, their fundamental premise is that "All is Mind," and when they so assert they place themselves in the direct line of inheritance with the teachings of the Vedanta and the still older schools of Hindu thought from which the Vedanta itself sprang. Idealistic Monism is older than recorded Hindu history, and undoubtedly had its origin among the earliest races on earth, the names and histories of which have passed from human memory. These "newest" thoughts of the so-called "New Thought" of the day are in reality *the very oldest thoughts of the race.* Verily, "there is nothing new under the sun."

BUDDHISM

Buddhism, that once popular philosophy of India, has now forsaken the land of its birth, and is almost unknown to the India of to-day, being represented by only a few northern tribes. In Burmah, Ceylon, Napal, Thibet, China, Japan, and other countries, however, the Buddhists hold their own and their followers are estimated at some 300,000,000 souls.

It is very difficult to explain the fundamental principles of Buddhism to the Western student, for his mind is not accustomed to considering *a Law without a Law-maker,* which idea underlies the Buddhistic thought. Buddhism has been called atheistic, by many Western writers, and atheistic it may be, for it certainly does not hold to the idea of a "God" in the Western understanding of that term. It holds rather to the idea of a Principle of Law which manifests in the countless and ever-changing shapes and forms and forces of the universe. At the last, however, Buddhism may be seen to hold to the existence of a Something, infinite, eternal, changeless, and indivisible, under, in, behind, and holding together the World of Change. This Something may be thought of either as Abstract Law, or else as Universal Will. But this Will is to be thought of merely as an abstract thing rather than as a thing of properties, qualities and attributes—*but possessing infinite possibilities of manifestation.* So, at the last, the Buddhist forms a conception of an Ultimate Reality which instead of being an Absolute Something is rather the Infinite Possibility of Everything. Rather a difficult conception for the average Western mind, but perfectly clear to the Oriental metaphysician! The Buddhist is accused of denying the existence of the soul—and so he does, in a way. He denies the existence of the individual soul as an independent and separate entity, but holds that it exists *as a temporary centre of consciousness* in the All. To the Buddhist all pain arises from this illusion of *separation and separateness,* and his aim is to overcome the illusion and to escape reincarnation, and once more to be absorbed into the One-All, "as the dew-drop slips into the shining sea." This Para-Nirvana—the Liberation, the Attainment!

The Buddhist does not indulge in much speculation regarding the nature of the Ultimate Reality—he regards it as unknowable, and thinks that all speculation regarding it is futile and a waste of time. Rather, he concerns himself with the Path of Attainment and Liberation—the escape from separateness and illusion. His spirit is well expressed by Edwin Arnold, in his "Light of Asia," as follows:

"Om, Amitaya! measure not with words
Th' Immeasurable; nor sink the string of thought
Into the Fathomless. Who asks doth err,
Who answers, errs. Say naught!
Shall any gazer see with mortal eyes,
Or any searcher know by mortal mind;

> Veil after veil will lift—but there must be
> Veil upon veil behind.
> The dew is on the Lotus!—Rise, Great Sun!
> And lift my leaf and mix me with the wave.
> *Om mani padme hum*, the Sunrise comes!
> The Dewdrop slips into the shining sea!"

Nirvana, the aim of every Buddhist in his earth-life, has been described by a Buddhistic writer as follows: "Nirvana is a condition of heart and mind in which every earthly craving is extinct; it is the cessation of every passion and desire, of every feeling of ill-will, fear and sorrow. It is a mental state of perfect rest and peace and joy, in the steadfast assurance of deliverance attained, from all the imperfections of finite being. It is a condition impossible to be defined in words, or to be conceived by anyone still attached to the things of the world. Only he knows what Nirvana is who has realized it in his own heart. It is deliverance, and is attainable in this life." What many Western writers describe as Nirvana is really the final stage called by the Buddhists "Para-Nirvana" in which the individual soul blends into the One Reality—when "the dew drop slips into the shining sea," and becomes one with the Infinite.

While the philosophy of Buddhism may be considered a negative one—the aim being a retreat rather than advance, or apparently so—still it has a high moral value, and advances moral ideals of the very highest. As Max Muller has said:

"The Buddha addressed himself to all castes and outcasts. He promised salvation to all, and he commanded his disciples to preach his doctrines in all places and to all men. A sense of duty, extending from the narrow limits of the house, the village, and the country, to the ardent circle of mankind; a feeling of sympathy and brotherhood to all men, the idea in fact of Humanity, *were first pronounced by Buddha.*"

But, although it has changed its dwelling place, Buddhism has left its influence upon Hindu thought, and its power is now manifesting itself in influencing the modern thought of the Western world. This has come about from various causes, chief among which is probably the influence of and general interest in modern Theosophy, the school established by Madame Blavatsky. To this influence must be added the popularity of the semi-Buddhistic conceptions of Schopenhauer and von Hartmann, in their idea of the World-Will, and the general leaning toward some of the original Buddhistic philosophical teachings on the part of certain modern scientists. Buddha's teaching that the Ultimate Reality is to be found only in a conception of a Universal Law, rather than in a Being, bears a striking analogy to the ideas of the Greek philosopher Heraclitus, and to the fundamental ideas of our modern philosopher, Herbert Spencer. Buddha's idea of the "Creative Will" which is ever striving to manifest itself in ever-changing phenomenal shape, form and variety, finds many modern followers in the philosophical school of "Voluntarism," the fundamental tenet of which is that "the ultimate nature of reality is to be conceived as some form of Will," a view specially favored by Schopenhauer and his followers.

The influence of Buddhism on modern Western thought is exerted through two channels, apparently unconnected, but still originally emerging from the same common source. Along one of these channels flows the stream of the Buddhistic doctrine of reincarnation (rebirth) and Karma (cause and effect operating in rebirth on the new life); along the other flows the stream of the doctrine of the power of Thought and Will. The first channel and its stream reaches the Western world through the fields claimed by Theosophy; the second wends its way through the somewhat diversified fields of the "New Thought" movement.

While the doctrine of reincarnation and Karma is firmly held by the orthodox Hindu schools of thought, it is nevertheless true that it finds its greatest growth and richest flowering in the Buddhistic garden. The Buddhists have reduced the doctrine of reincarnation and Karma to a science, and the ordinary Hindu presentation seems tame and subdued by comparison. The conceptions entertained by Theosophy, so far as this particular doctrine is concerned, were obtained directly from Buddhist sources. Madame Blavatsky's writings on reincarnation and Karma bear the impress of Buddhism, and still more plainly does the mark show on Mr.

Sinnett's statement of the doctrine in his "Esoteric Buddhism;" while Col. Olcott, one of the founders of the Theosophical Society, lived and died an ardent Buddhist. Theosophy itself, while it has outgrown some of the limitations of Buddhism and has moved into the general field of Hindu and ancient Greek thought, must acknowledge its indebtedness to Buddhism for its (Theosophy's) cardinal doctrines of reincarnation and Karma. And the general interest in these subjects manifested of late years in Western thought may be readily traced to the school of Gautama, the Buddha.

Reincarnation, as every reader probably knows, is the doctrine of repeated rebirth in the physical body—the soul being held to have risen by degrees from the lowest animal forms, thence incarnating in a succession of human bodies, during many lives and personalities, from whence it shall eventually move forward to higher forms of life, until finally it shall enter into the blissful state of Nirvana, bliss and freedom from rebirth. The term "Nirvana" is distinctly Buddhistic, the Hindu equivalent being "Moksha," meaning liberation, emancipation, divine absorption, etc. Karma is the doctrine accompanying that of reincarnation, and the term means "The law of spiritual cause and effect," the workings of which determine the successive incarnations of the individual soul. Each act is held to generate Karma, or the "seed of future action" which will sprout, grow, blossom and bear fruit in future lives. Karma is akin to fate, but a fate arising from one's own actions, thoughts and deeds, rather than imposed by providence.

It is interesting to notice how the idea of reincarnation and Karma has grown in the minds of Western people during the past two decades. Originally repugnant to the Western mind, it has nevertheless managed to work its way to an acceptance on the part of many people who are searching for the new in philosophy and religion. It is now quite common to hear people discussing the probability of their having lived before the present life, and accounting for many of the happenings, joyful or sorrowful, of the present life, upon the basis of Karma.

The other channel of Buddhistic thought, through which is flowing a stream which is irrigating the Western lands, is that which is bringing about the remarkable interest in thought-force, will-power, etc., now noticeable on all sides. While the orthodox Hindu schools recognize the power of thought-force and will, they are too much taken up with the dreamy, transcendental, metaphysical speculations to bestow more than a passing notice to the subject. Not so with the Buddhist! The Buddhist priesthood, in Thibet, Ceylon, and in Japan, particularly, have devoted much time and study to the subject of the thought-force and will. They have evolved a distinctively Buddhistic psychology, of which the general Western world knows little. Chief among their beliefs is that thought-force and will are dynamic forces, capable of being employed for good or evil, and which are operative over a distance. The phenomena of hypnotism, telepathy, mental control, mental influence, mental fascination, etc., are quite familiar to the Buddhists, and are taught in their inner schools. The will is held to be the governing power, to which all else is subordinate.

This so-called "practical" side of the Oriental philosophy, which proves so attractive to the Western mind, is distinctively Buddhistic in its origin and source—although belonging to the "occult" side of Buddhism, and not to the philosophic, religious, ethical or moral sides.

ZOROASTRIANISM

The great school of Oriental religio-philosophical thought known as "Zoroastrianism" was founded by Zoroaster (or Zarathushtra), the great teacher of ancient Iran or Persia, who is believed to have lived about 700 B. C., that period of Oriental history in which was manifested the great revival of religio-philosophic thought, and which marked the founding of several great schools of Oriental philosophy and religion. Zoroaster's philosophy sprang into immediate popularity, and at one time exerted a dominating influence over the minds and lives of millions of people. At present it has almost entirely disappeared, its death-blow having been dealt by the rise of the school of Mohammed, and to-day it is represented chiefly by scattered groups of Parsees or Fire-Worshippers.

But although it has almost entirely disappeared from the active scene, its influence in the past has been great, and its teachings continue to-day, in other religions and philosophies. Zoroastrianism, once one of the world's greatest religions and philosophies, was undermined by the blows dealt by Alexander the Great, and afterward almost destroyed by the Moslem conquerers. To-day it exists merely as a memory, with but a few hundred thousand followers of its modern phases. But its influence has been great, inasmuch as it has supplied vital material for other faiths and beliefs, the majority of which are ignorant of their debt to the old Persian teacher. A wreck on the shores of time, its material has been used to build many modern ships of faith now sailing the sea of religious thought with swelling sails and fluttering pennants. Or, changing the figure, I may say that although its flame is now flickering but feebly, and threatens soon to die out entirely, yet from it many other torches have been lighted—many fires kindled—so that it lives, and will live in the time to come, under many strange names and in many new forms.

Prof. Jackson has said: "As a rule, the ideality and lofty spirituality of Zoroaster's teachings have been generally recognized; and the efficiency of the faith as a working religion may be seen in the fruits which it has borne in various ways through history, and in its present followers, the Parsees and Ghebers. Haug has said: "We must class Zoroaster among the real benefactors of the human race." Mills says: "Zoroastrianism was the faith of many millions of human beings throughout successive generations. . . . If the mental illumination and spiritual elevation of many millions of mankind through long periods of time are of any importance, it would require strong proof to deny that Zoroastrianism has had an influence of very positive power in determining the gravest results." West says: "Zoroaster was the founder of a pure and sublime religion based upon the eternal principle of right and wrong, good and evil, light and darkness, and he was far in advance of any teacher of which human annals have preserved a record." Laing says: "It is evident that this simple and sublime religion is one to which, by whatever name we may call it, modern science is fast approximating. Men of science like Huxley, philosophers like Herbert Spencer, poets like Tennyson, might subscribe to it. The Encyclopædia Brittanica says: "Zoroaster's teachings show him to have been a man of highly speculative turn, faithful, however, with all his originality, to the Iranian national character. With zeal for the faith, and boldness and energy, he combined diplomatic skill in his dealings with his exalted protectors. His thinking is consecutive, self-restrained, practical, devoid, on the whole, of what may be called fantastic and excessive. His form of expression is tangible and concrete. His system is constructed on a clearly conceived plan."

Zoroastrianism may be said to base its teachings upon the following fundamental principles:

I. That there exists one eternal principle, called *Zaruana Akarana*, which name freely translated means, "eternal." This principle is regarded as purely *abstract, unknowable, unthinkable, and unspeakable.*

II. From this eternal principle is held to have proceeded, simultaneously, the twin-principles of good and evil, known respectively as *Ahura Mazda*, or "Ormuzd" (the principle of good); and *Anra Mainyu*, or "Ahriman," (the principle of evil). Ormuzd created light, health, truth, and all "good" things; Ahriman created darkness, disease, lies, and all "bad" things. In short, these two principles represent the conception of God and Devil, so common in later religious systems.

III. When Ormuzd and Ahriman first met, and time thus began, there arose a mighty struggle between the respective principles of good and evil, which still continues. During the first three thousand years the fight was on the spiritual plane. Ahriman arising from his abyss of darkness was dazzled by the light of Ormuzd, and was driven back. But gathering around him his hellish clan, he renewed the attack. The second three thousand years was marked by the creation of the universe and man, by Ormuzd, in order that he might defeat Ahriman. But during the third three thousand years, Ahriman, the serpent-like being, invaded the world, and tempting man mingled evil with good, and introduced sin in the world in order to corrupt the race of man and thus bring to naught the work of Ormuzd. Zoroaster taught *that we are now in this second period of the conflict, with Ahriman in the ascendant.* The conflict is now raging fiercely, Ormuzd being assisted by his hosts of angelic creatures, and Ahriman being followed by a horde of devilish creatures—the legions of heaven and hell meeting and being engaged in constant conflict for the possession of the universe and the souls of men. The world is now suffering, pain, evil, sin and disease from the misrule of Ahriman, yet ever struggling toward good and Ormuzd. The teaching is that a fourth period of three thousand years is approaching, when man, seeing the value of good, will come to the aid of Ormuzd, and turning the tide of battle will defeat Ahriman and his devils, and binding them, will hurl them down to the bottomless abyss of darkness. Thereupon, in this "millenium," good, light, truth and health will be the possession of the race.

All of which has a very familiar sound to the ears of the Western reader, has it not? By many of the students of the Higher Criticism, the book of Job (which is distinctively non-Hebraic) is believed to have been derived from Zoroastrian, or pre-Zoroastrian, sources. And, students of comparative religion have long been familiar with the striking resemblance between certain portions of the book of Revelations and the Zoroastrian teachings, the latter ante-dating the former by seven centuries. Moreover, it is claimed by careful students of the subject that many of the ceremonials, holy-days, etc., of Mithraism (a branch of Zoroastrianism) were incorporated into the early Christian church during the first two or three centuries of its existence. Other religions have been materially influenced by this almost forgotten religio-philosophy of the past.

Zoroaster's moral teachings were excellent. His Triad summed up the law as follows: I. *Humata,* or good thoughts; II. *Huxta,* or good words; and III. *Hvarsta,* or good deeds. He taught universal brotherhood and universal kindness to all, irrespective of race, country or creed. Kindness to animals was enjoined. Personal cleanliness was made a religious duty. Work, likewise, was held to be a religious duty and virtue, the tilling of the soil being regarded as a sacred work. Zoroaster's 'Golden

Rule" was: "Think of, speak to, and act toward your brothers (and all men are your brothers), as you would desire that they should think of, speak to, and act toward you."

SUFIISM

Sufiism is the mystic and inner-teaching found within the body of the Mohammedan religion, principally in Persia and Arabia. It undoubtedly existed long before the time of Mohammed, and is believed to have been incorporated in the religion of the Prophet in order that it might not be destroyed by his conquering faith. The legends are that Ali, the favorite disciple of Mohammed, was a Sufi, and managed to save his mystic faith by persuading the Prophet to admit it into the new religion as an inner-teaching. The Sufis have a legend which relates that "The seed of Sufiism was sown in the time of Adam; germinated in the time of Noah; budded in the time of Abraham; began to develop in the time of Jesus; and produced pure wine in the time of Mohammed." The term "Sufi" is derived from the Persian word *"suf,"* meaning "wool," its use arising from the fact that the ancient Sufi teachers wore a single garment of undyed and unbleached wool.

Sufiism has exerted its principal influence upon the thought of the outside world by reason of its poetry. Nearly all of the great Persian and Arabian poets have been Sufis, and have woven in their mystic religion by veiled metaphors, the terms "wine," the "vine," the "grape," and also the "rose," the "nightingale," the "beloved one," and similar terms familiar in Oriental poetry, having a mystic significance. Briefly, it may be said that in the Sufi poetry, such terms as "the grape," "the wine," "the vine," etc., have reference to the mystic teaching of the Sufis; while terms such as "the beloved," "the damsel," "the rose," refer to the Sufi conception of the Divine One, "the lover" and "the nightingale" being the Sufi worshipper. As for instance this verse from Omar Khayyam, who was a Sufi:

"And David's lips are lockt; but in divine
High-piping Pehlevi, with Wine! Wine! Wine!
Red Wine!—the Nightingale cries to the Rose
That sallow-cheek of her's to incarnadine."

Or this verse from Jalal-ud-Din Rumi:

"The souls love-moved are circling on,
Like streams to their great Ocean-King.
Thou art the Sun of all men's thoughts;
Thy kisses are the flowers of Spring.
The dawn is pale from yearning Love;
The moon in tears is sorrowing.
Thou art the Rose, and deep for Thee,
In sighs, the Nightingales still sing."

Sufiism may be described as *an absolute idealistic monism, tinged with a devout and fervent mysticism.* An authority says: "Sufiism is the mystical and pantheistic doctrine of the Sufis. They consider that

God alone exists; that He is in all nature, and that all nature is in Him, the visible universe being an emanation from His essence." The fundamental principles of the Sufis may be simply stated in these words: *God is all there is; besides Him there is naught; the universe is but a reflection or idea in the mind of God, and has no existence outside of Him.*

To the Sufi the universe is a great stage upon which is enacted the eternal drama of life, in which the Divine One creates, moves, and then destroys the characters and the scenery—all being but mental creations and existing but in His mind. Old Omar Khayyam, that much misunderstood Sufi poet, states this in bold simplicity in his *Rubaiyat*, when he sings:

"Whose secret presence, through Creation's veins
Running Quicksilver-like eludes your pains;
Taking all shapes from Mah to Mahi; and
They change and perish all—but HE remains;
A moment guessed—then back behind the Fold
Immerst of Darkness round the Drama rolled
Which, for the pastime of Eternity,
He doth Himself contrive, enact, behold."

"We are no other than a moving row
Of Magic Shadow-shapes that come and go
Round with the Sun-illumined Lantern held
In Midnight by the Master of the Show;
But helpless Pieces of the Game He plays
Upon His Chequer-board of Nights and Days:
Hither and Thither moves, and checks and slays,
And one by one back in the Closet lays.

> The Ball no question makes of Ayes and Noes,
> But Here and There, as strikes the Player, goes;
> And He that tossed you down into the Field,
> He knows about it all—He knows—HE knows!"

But this pessimistic and apparently hopeless outlook upon life does not bring terror to the soul of the Sufi. While recognizing that the universe is but an illusion, and life but a puppet-show, he remembers that *if God is all there is, then the individual must be a part of or phase of God*—and toward the union with God he bends all his soul and life. Discarding the sugar-plum reward of heavenly bliss in future worlds, as taught in the Mohammedan creed, he seeks to fly straight to the heart of Being, and seeks his comfort and security there in the bosom of God.

The Sufi is a true mystic, and seeks ever for the union with The Beloved One. He strives to enter into conscious union with God here in earth-life; and hopes for absorption in God in the future when his soul leaves the body. He leaves the thousand heavens of the orthodox Mohammedan—he will have none of them—but piercing through the illusion which embraces even the highest heavens, like the arrow to the mark, or the homing-pigeon to its nest, he flies straight to the embrace of the Beloved. During his life-time, he indulges in meditations, reveries, and "silences"—he also favors sacred dances to slow music accompanied by rhythmic movements of the body. He feels strange longings of the soul, which he holds to be dim memories of his previous blissful state in the bosom of the One, and the natural craving to return thereto. He believes that his ideas of the good, the beautiful, and the true, are but memories of his previous bliss. He believes in fate and destiny, but holds them to be but the Divine stage-machinery in the drama of the universe. His soul is ever home-sick for the One. And, in this spirit, Avicenna, the Sufi poet, sings of the mourning soul, sighing over its loss, and longing for its home-journey and return to its Beloved:

"Lo, it was hurled
'Midst the sign posts and ruined abodes of this blessed world.
It weeps, when it thinks of its home, and the peace it possessed,
With tears welling forth from its eyes without pausing or rest,
And with plaintive mourning it broodeth like one bereft
O'er such trace of its home as the fourfold winds have left."

And, so, with constant faith and ardent hope lives on the Sufi, seeking ever the path which leads to union. Perplexed not by the speculations of the theologians and the philosophers, he answers simply:

"He knows about it all—He knows—HE knows!"

And who among us can dispute his wisdom?

CHAPTER IX

WESTERN PHILOSOPHIES

In the preceding chapters we have traced certain tendencies in modern thought back to the Transcendental Movement of which Emerson was the high priest and prophet; thence back to the philosophies of ancient Greece; and thence back to the Oriental philosophies. We must now begin our return journey to the present time. But in order to lend variety to the trip, and in order to become acquainted with the other roads which lead to the Rome of modern thought, we shall forsake the path of transcendentalism over which we traveled on our outward journey, and shall return home by the road of the Western philosophers. This road, like that of Transcendentalism, extends from the schools of old India, via ancient Greece, to the schools of popular modern thought in the Western world of the twentieth century.

By the term "the Western philosophers" I wish to indicate the leaders and pioneers of philosophical thought from, say, the beginning of the seventeenth century to the present time. Before the Western philosophers, and after the Grecian philosophers, came the school of Patristic Philosophy, beginning at about the second century, the teachers of which were the Fathers of the Church. The Patristic Philosophy was in the nature of an effort to reconcile the early Christian theology with the older Grecian philosophical conceptions, Neo-Platonism and Gnosticism playing an important part in the intellectual struggle.

After the Patristic School came that of the Scholastic Philosophy, the central figure of the division being St. Augustine, who died 430 A. D. The Scholastic Philosophy was a strange mingling of medieval philosophical thought under the domination of the orthodox theology, having for its aim the exposition of the dogmas of the church in the terminology of rational philosophical inquiry. This school was characterized by extreme and often excessive subtlety of expression and refinement of reasoning, and "the making of formal distinctions without end and without special point." As an authority says: "Scholasticism was the reproduction of ancient philosophy under the control of the ecclesiastical discipline, the former being accommodated to the latter, in case of any discrepancy between them." The first period of the Scholastic Philosophy extended to the beginning of the thirteenth century, at which time the influence of the old Aristotelian philosophy began to reassert itself by reason of the appearance of the writings of Aristotle in Western Europe. The second period of the Scholastic Philosophy extended from this time until the Renaissance in the fifteenth century, and was marked by the adaptation of the whole Aristotelian philosophy to orthodox theology, the doctrine of Aristotle becoming the basis of the theoretical philosophy of the Church. The "high-water mark" of Scholasticism was in the early part of the fourteenth century.

THE RENAISSANCE

Succeeding the Scholastic Philosophy came that of the Renaissance—that remarkable period of the transition from the thought of the middle ages to that of modern times—that strange reawakening or rebirth of thought, art and letters. This period extended over the fifteenth and sixteenth centuries. The philosophy of the Renaissance was notable for the marked revival of the influence of Plato in Neo-Platonism, which, as usual, resulted in breaking up the crystallized forms of orthodox philosophy and theology, and giving to thought the tinge of mysticism and transcendentalism. Neo-Platonism seems to reappear at regular intervals of time in philosophical thought, and always with a disturbing influence. It is now manifesting in modern thought, in the usual way, as we have seen in the preceding chapters of this work. At the time of the Renaissance it served to break and disintegrate the Scholastic Philosophy, and fitted in with the trend toward the study of nature's processes which the thought of that time had begun to favor. As an authority says:

"Platonism flourished in the Academy of Florence . . . Neo-Platonism blended with Neo-Pythagoreanism. . . . Aristotelianism renewed its vigor in the two rival schools of Averroism and Alexandrism, and among the Protestants in Melanchton." The disturbances in thought at the time of the Renaissance were very similar to that of the present time, and the two periods invite comparison and comparative study.

What I have called "The Western Philosophies" sprang from the fertile soil of the Renaissance, and by the beginning of the seventeenth century was showing blossom and bearing fruit. I think that I can give a better view of the various influences at work from that time on by asking you to consider briefly the ideas and teachings of the representative teachers of the period, rather than to treat the thought as a whole. So many conflicting elements appear that it is difficult to consider it in the latter way.

THE BACONIAN PHILOSOPHY

Perhaps it would be best to begin the story of the Western philosophers by a consideration of Francis Bacon, that brilliant though eccentric genius, whose power is becoming manifest more clearly as time passes. Francis Bacon was an Englishman, who lived A. D. 1561-1629. At Cambridge he became disgusted with Aristotle's philosophy, which was accepted almost as final by many of the thinkers of the time. He laid the foundation of modern empiricism, or the doctrine *that truth is to be sought in actual experience.* He opposed the deductive or *a priori* speculations of the Scholastics—the speculations which from an assumed general principle, or explanation, proceeded to particular truths—and favored the reasoning which, from actual facts gathered by experience, proceeded to general principles resulting from the same. He insisted that instead of nature being studied from theories or dogmas concerning the Divine Nature it should be known by an examination of her phenomena, without bias, and that possibly even ultimate truth itself might be ascertained from this knowledge of facts of experience. The "Baconian Method" is defined as "The method of investigating experience which proceeds from given particular facts, and applies to general conceptions that have not themselves been gained from and tested by comparison with particulars." This method of reasoning laid the basis for the scientific discoveries which have followed, and did much to direct thought toward physics and away from metaphysics, in its search for truth. An authority says: "The great triumphs of modern science have arisen from a resolute adherence on the part of its votaries to the Baconian method of inquiry." Another says: "It is the Baconian spirit of going direct to nature, and verifying our opinions and theories by experiment, that has led to all the great discoveries of modern science." And it is Bacon's spirit which has caused the change in metaphysical and philosophical thought, compelling it to take scientific facts and experience into consideration in arriving at general principles, instead of boldly assuming the general principle as truth, and then attempting to account for the phenomena of nature in accordance with the assumed principle. The philosophy of to-day must be based upon observed facts and items of experience. For this we have Bacon to thank.

BRUNO

Giordano Bruno, an Italian philosopher, who lived A. D. 1548-1600, exerted a lasting influence on later philosophy, although his name has never been accorded its true place in the history of philosophy. He was originally a priest, but was driven out of the church by reason of his philosophical views, and finally was burned at the stake by the Inquisition when he refused to recant. A statue, erected by his modern admirers, now stands upon the exact place of his execution in Rome, where it was erected in spite of the protests of the Vatican. His philosophy was a mystic pantheism, with a poetical personification of nature. He held that there is an All-Life, animating the whole universe, which thus is seen to be an universal living being. This universal living being has two aspects, the one called *natura naturans,* or God, who manifests himself in the visible world of phenomena, which is called *natura naturata,* or nature. He held that in God all the seeming inconsistencies of the material world are harmonized, and the apparent evil becomes good. He held that every part of the universe is animated with the life of the whole, and that there is no dead or non-living thing in the world. He held that there is no form without matter, and that as spirit or soul is the essence of form, it could manifest only in material embodiment. His philosophy exerted a marked influence on later modern pantheistic or naturalistic thought, and also upon the systems of Descartes, Spinoza, Boehme, Hegel and others, and in a measure upon the latest conceptions of monistic thought in evidence at the present time.

THE CARTESIAN PHILOSOPHY

René Descartes was a French philosopher, who lived A. D. 1596-1650. He is often called "the father of modern philosophy." He was reared in a Jesuit college, but became dissatisfied with the prevailing teachings of Scholasticism, and determined to abandon books and to clear his mind of what he had learned, and then begin his philosophical thought afresh. Discarding everything, he found that Thought still remained, and that he was conscious of his own existence, or the awareness of "I Am."

Thus arose his famous proposition, "I *think,* therefore I *am.*" Inquiring next into ideas, or "all that is in our mind when we conceive a thing, in whatever way we conceive it," he regarded clearness and distinctness as the criterion of the true as distinguished from the false. He held that the clearest idea in the human mind is the idea of God; therefore, there must be a God. Similarly he reasoned that God must be an absolutely perfect being, and that such a being could not deceive us in mathematical and metaphysical reasoning faculties, and that therefore these sciences must be trustworthy. From this he reasoned that the actual existence of the phenomenal world is proved by the prior truth of the existence of God. He held that there exists spirit and matter —thinking and extended substance—and that creation was and is a manifestation of divine will. He was practically the founder of the modern school of Rationalism, or the doctrine that reason is an independent source of knowledge, distinct from sense perception, and having a higher authority; and that in philosophy, certain elementary concepts are to be sought, and that the remaining principles of philosophy may be deduced from these fundamental notions. His philosophy was very popular during the latter half of the seventeenth and the whole of the eighteenth century. His ideas were developed by Spinoza and Leibnitz, and were finally refuted by Kant, who held that from concepts could be deduced only that which had previously been put in them, and that rational concepts must be applied to the material of sense gained through experience. Rationalism, however, still exists in philosophy in a modified form, even Kant, who gave it its death blow as a perfect method, endeavoring to combine its truths with those of Empiricism, or the doctrine that truth is to be sought only through experience.

SPINOZA

Baruch Spinoza, a Dutch Jew, who lived A. D. 1632-1677, was one of the greatest philosophers of modern times. Excommunicated from the Jewish faith, and persecuted in many ways, he supported himself by grinding lenses. His character was admirable, and he stands out in history as one of the most sincere and consistent of philosophers. His system was a complicated pantheism. He held that all things were of one Substance, and that that Substance existed independently of any external cause or power—consequently that Substance must be God. By Substance, however, Spinoza did not mean matter or material principle, but the underlying reality, or the self-sufficient and comprehensive basis for, or essence of, all reality, capable at the same time of manifesting as its attributes all temporal and phenomenal existence. He held to the possibility of an infinite number of attributes in Substance, but that only two kinds were known to us, namely: The attribute of extension, or matter; and the attribute of thinking, or mind. These two attributes were held to be parallel manifestations or attributes of the hidden substantial reality of God. All particular things, psychical or physical, are "modes" of God, according to Spinoza, and bear the same relation to him as does the stream to the ocean, or time to eternity. God, he held, was the *natura naturans,* and nature the *natura naturata*—the one the energy, the other the act. The "modes" he held to be ephemeral, while God is eternal, outlasting all changes of time or space. He taught that only by identification with the eternal verities, with Substance, with God, can immortality, or peace, be obtained. Spinoza founded no school, but his spirit lives in nearly all philosophies since his time; even Haeckel, the modern scientific monistic authority, freely acknowledges his indebtedness to the Jewish philosopher. Spinoza's spirit is evidenced in his axiom: "To define God is to deny him." Lewes says of him: "Neither in Holland nor in Germany has there been a Spinozist, as there have been Cartesians, Kantists and Hegelians, although German philosophy is in some sense saturated with Spinozism."

LEIBNITZ

Gottfried Wilhelm von Leibnitz was a German philosopher, who lived A. D. 1646-1716. He was influenced largely by Descartes regarding the doctrine of innate ideas; by Spinoza regarding rationalism; and by Locke regarding individualism. He held that nothing comes to the soul from without, but that all knowledge is merely an unfoldment of ideas originally possessed and innate, as "the small, dark notions of the soul"—all ideas are innate and not acquired, although the explicit consciousness of them is acquired. He holds to an infinite Substance, but breaks its unity up into an infinite number of monads—his reality exists in itself, but acts through its monads. The monads, or souls, he holds, have the whole universe mirrored in themselves. The nature of each monad is held to be the same, but they vary infinitely in their degrees of perception, the most obscure perception belonging to the monads which we call matter. While God is pure activity, the finite monads are in a state of imperfect realization, the passivity of the finite monads giving rise to the illusion of the material world. He held that God is the "Monad of monads," and his influence causes the changes of the finite monads to harmonize. Leibnitz was a radical optimist, holding that the universe was the best of all possible universes, having been selected as such by God by reason of His infinite wisdom and goodness. He did not assert that the universe was perfect, but that as a whole the world was the best of all possible worlds, and that for this reason God was justified for selecting a world in which there was evil. The followers of Leibnitz sacrificed his fundamental principles, as above stated, and held merely to his rationalistic methods, the result being to reduce the philosophy to its Scholastic form. The result was the decline of dogmatic rationalism. A new school, that of Empiricism, was beginning to wage war on the rationalists, and a new era in philosophy was dawning.

LOCKE

John Locke was an English philosopher who lived A. D. 1632-1704. He was the founder of the modern school of philosophy known as Empiricism, the principal doctrine of which is that *all knowledge or truth is to be obtained only through experience,* as opposed to the "theory of innate ideas." Locke developed the Baconian idea that experience was the true source of knowledge, and that general truths should be reasoned inductively from observed facts of experience. He held that in empirical facts we may find the only source of knowledge, since the mind has no innate ideas. His teaching was that the materials for thought and reason are impressed upon the mind from outside, and that the sole activity of the mind is that of linking and combining together the ideas so obtained. He argued from this that our knowledge of the external world, resting, as it does, upon sense-perception, must be merely upon the plane of probability. He, however, violated his fundamental principle by assuming a rationalistic ideal including the assertion that we have an intuitive knowledge of the existence of the self, the existence of God, and of mathematical and moral truths. While under the influence of Bacon, he was nevertheless largely influenced by the rationalism of Descartes. While apparently advancing the full doctrine of empiricism, he managed to point out the way for its reconciliation with rationalism, which way was pursued by Kant in after years.

HUME

David Hume, a Scotch philosopher (A. D. 1711-1776), afterward carried Locke's fundamental theories to their logical conclusion, and held that there was naught knowable other than conscious experiences; that is, "impressions" and their reflection, "ideas." Hume held that we cannot transcend this knowledge, although we may combine the ideas by association, etc., according to the established principles of psychology. Hume taught that we cannot prove the existence of God, of self, or of matter—all of which ideas are the illusions of imagination, having no basis in actual experience. He carried empiricism to the realm of pure skepticism.

BERKELEY

George Berkeley was a bishop of the Church of England, who lived A. D. 1685-1753. He was the founder of the modern school of Idealism, which system he developed largely upon the basis of Locke, Descartes, Spinoza and Leibnitz. He held that matter cannot be conceived to actually exist, the only real substance being mind; and that the material world is nothing but a complex of mental impressions which appear and disappear in accordance with established laws of nature. He held that the reality of sense objects consisted in their being perceived, and that the assumption of an object apart from its idea is fallacious. He denied the individual existence of object apart from the subjective idea of it, and of both subject and object apart from the mind of God, or the Absolute. He held that, there being no real external world, the phenomena of sense must depend upon God continually, necessitating perception. Berkeley set out to prove the existence of God by his idealistic theory, but reasoned in a circle when he assumed the existence of God to make his theory tenable. His opponents endeavored to confute him by the familiar illustration of one kicking a stone and realizing the reality of the effect produced, but he and his followers logically explained that the said effect was merely a sensation known by the mind, and not a thing outside of the mind. Idealism, in various forms, has permeated many later philosophical systems. Fichte, Schelling and Hegel have made the doctrine parts of their respective systems, and it is heard from in the metaphysical systems and theories of to-day.

KANT

Immanuel Kant, the great German philosopher, lived A. D. 1724-1804. His work created a new era in modern philosophy, and has profoundly affected all subsequent philosophical thought, even in systems which are apparently opposed to his fundamental principles. He was the founder of the modern school of Critical Philosophy. He, following the skepticism of Hume as to the idea of causality, enunciated the proposition that the faculty of knowledge, and the sources of knowledge, must be critically examined before anything could be definitely determined regarding objective truth. He aimed to separate the intuitive, or *a priori* mental forms, from those obtained empirically, or through experience; and also to define and determine the limits of human reason and the knowledge obtained therefrom. He attributed to the faculties of sense, understanding, judgment and reason, certain innate ideas, intuitive truths, or *a priori* forms, which must be valid and real because of their necessity, as, for instance, the ideas of time and space, cause and effect, action and reaction, reality, unity, the idea of the Absolute, and certain moral truths, such as his famous "categorical imperative" which held as axiomatic the idea that one should "Act only on that maxim whereby thou canst at the same time will that it should become a universal law"—the latter being claimed by him to be a moral law which admits of no condition or exception.

He held that theoretical knowledge was limited, inasmuch as the universal ideas existing in the mind would yield knowledge only when excited thereto by the presentation of their corresponding objects in actual experience, and that even then what we really know is not the "thing-in-itself," but merely the "thing-as-it-appears"—the phenomenon, not the *noumenon.* The result of his reasoning is that certain "things-in-themselves" must be unknowable, as they can never appear to the mind as objects of actual experience in consciousness, and are to be thought of only as belonging to the *noumenal*, or the world of "things-in-themselves." These unknowable things are the transcendental thought-postulates in psychology, cosmology, and theology, as, for instance, "God, freedom, and immortality of the soul," and the "opposites" or contradictions which reason meets in considering the ideas of infinity, as infinite time, infinite space, infinite chain of cause and effect. As an authority says of Kant's teachings: "His point is that though it is unquestionably necessary to be convinced of God's existence, it is not so necessary to demonstrate it. . . . He shows that all such demonstrations are scientifically impossible and worthless. On the great questions of metaphysics—immortality, freedom, God—scientific knowledge is hopeless."

It will be seen that Kant ambitiously essayed to harmonize and blend the opposing principles of rationalism and empiricism—of *a priori* and *a posteriori* knowledge—of innate ideas and ideas arising from experience. He held that knowledge is composed of two factors, as follows: (1) *A priori*, innate in the mind itself, antedating experience and necessary to make experience possible; and (2) *a posteriori*, coming from without, as the raw material of sensation, through experience. He held that the *a priori* knowledge is not usable without the material of sense experience; and that the *a posteriori* knowledge would fail to take form in consciousness were it not for the mold ideas innately existing in the mind. He held, therefore, that while theoretical reason or scientific inquiry is necessarily limited to the realm of experience and phenomenon, still practical reason is valid in postulating belief in the moral law and order, and belief in the existence of a world of transcendental reality. "Practical reason," he held, made it necessary for us to postulate the existence of "God, freedom, and immortality," and to manifest our belief in our moral life, although "pure reason" was absolutely unable to demonstrate their existence. Thus did Kant endeavor to build a structure of faith upon a foundation of reason.

HEGEL

George Wilhelm Friedrich Hegel, who lived A. D. 1770-1831, was one of the greatest and most influential of the modern German philosophers. His philosophy is known as that of Absolute Idealism. It is almost impossible to state his philosophy in popular terms, and in a limited space, so subtle and complicated is his thought and so voluminous the expression thereof. The following brief synopsis, therefore, must be accepted only with the above understanding. Hegel was a Rationalist of the most extreme type, although his expression differed from that of the English philosophers of that school, and his conceptions blended Rationalism with Idealism in a striking manner. He held that reality is but a manifestation of mind, and mind a manifestation of reality. The universe, he held, is the product of thought, and its life and activities are those of thought—nature is "petrified intelligence." History, he held, is but the record of the process of absolute spirit toward complete self-realization. Mind, or reason, is all there is—"the real is rational and the rational is real," he said. He held that in knowing "what is" we knew reason, for reason is all "that is." He held that progress, in reality, is an illusion, and that "the consummation of the infinite end consists merely in removing the illusion which makes it seem still unaccomplished . . . the idea makes itself that illusion by setting up an antithesis to confront itself, and its acting consists in getting rid of the illusion which it has created." He also held that the motive force of the world-development was "opposition and negation"—everything is what it is by reason of what it is not, and everything, therefore, "both is and is not" at the same time, and can be understood only by combining the "is" and the "is not" in a higher synthesis. But he is careful to state, the contradictories are not annulled when combined, but are merely conserved—though when thus conserved they are no longer contradictory. By this process of reasoning, Hegel held that Being and Not-Being are one—from a union of and conservation of these two contradictories he obtained the idea of "Becoming." After Hegel's death his followers divided into opposing schools, each claiming to truly represent his thought, although diametrically opposed to each other. To such radical extremes was Hegelism carried by his followers that his system fell into disfavor in Germany, although at present it is experiencing a revival in England and America under the name of Neo-Hegelism, and in some of the "New Thought" cults.

SCHOPENHAUER

Arthur Schopenhauer, the German philosopher, who was an active opponent, philosophically and personally, of Hegel, lived A. D. 1788-1860. To many he is known as the apostle of pessimism, although his general philosophy has attracted great attention, particularly in Germany. His general philosophy is known as Voluntarism, or the doctrine that ultimate reality is to be conceived of as an universal will, instead of an universal reason. He held that reality, or the universal "Thing-in-Itself," is the principle of will, which manifests itself in various degrees and phases as physical, chemical, magnetic and vital force in nature, its most striking phase, however, being the "Will-to-Live" which manifests through all living forms, seeking expression and objective life. The "Will-to-Live," he held, is instinctive rather than rational, and acts as "blind nature" in the struggles to perpetuate life, in the struggle for existence and the reproduction of the species. He claimed that the instinct of self-preservation and of sexual attraction is but the urge of the "Will-to-Live" seeking channels of expression. He held that reason is merely a "by-product" of Will—an excrescence, so to speak—and that reason cannot expect to apprehend reality, for the latter is Will. The force of intellect, he holds, is inferior to that of the Will, and is subordinated to the latter, eventually, whenever, as often happens, the two come in conflict. In Will, he claims, we view nature from the inside, while in intellect we view her from the outside. The phenomenal world he regards as merely "presentation" to the Will—in fact, an illusion similar to the *Maya* of the Hindus. Schopenhauer, in fact, was a Western Buddhist, and his philosophy follows that latter school in many essential details.

Schopenhauer held that the World-Spirit, which he calls Will, does not act according to reason, but rather by caprice instigated by a desire or lust for expression. His Will is ever at work building up; tearing down; replacing; repairing; changing—always at work—always acting—always doing. It is ever filled with intense longing to express itself into shape and form and force—ever desiring *change*. Finally it develops self-consciousness and reason in man, and then turns its gaze inward upon itself, studying its own nature through man's philosophy and metaphysics. In man the instinctive Will rises to reason, and for the first time is able to control its own instinctive nature. In creating intellect the Will forges an instrument destined to master and conquer itself.

This, briefly, is Schopenhauer's conception of the World-Spirit, derived largely from Buddhistic sources, and destined to play an important part in later Western thought.

VON HARTMANN

Edward von Hartmann (1842-1906), the German philosopher, built largely upon Schopenhauer's foundation, although differing from him greatly in his final conclusions. He accepted Schopenhauer's idea of the World-Spirit, ever at work building up and tearing down—ever seeking change in shape, form and manifestation of force—but he held that the conception of Will without rational idea was illogical and unthinkable, just as Hegel's conception of rational idea without Will was illogical. He thereupon, seeks to harmonize and reconcile the two conceptions. He postulates the existence of a World-Spirit in which Will and rational idea are combined as the two phases, or two poles, just as the color and perfume of the rose are complementary and essential. But he holds that the rational idea phase of the World Spirit is unconscious, and, in fact, he applies the term "the unconscious" to his conception of the World-Spirit. This unconscious spirit he pictures as using its powers of ideation and Will in the work of objective manifestation, ever at work creating new shapes and forms, and manifesting change and variety. Like a somnambulist it proceeds with its work, according to logical ideas, instinctively but according to the laws of rationality. Finally the unconscious manifests consciousness, and then self-consciousness in man, and may even proceed to higher forms of consciousness in higher beings yet to be evolved. But, in itself, it is unconscious and must ever remain so, its only consciousness being obtained through its created manifestations. Such is von Hartmann's conception of the unconscious World-Spirit. His conception of unconscious mind has been used, often without due credit, but later writers and investigators of the "subliminal mind;" the "subjective mind;" the "subconscious mind;" etc., in man. It is very probable that his philosophy will be developed in greater detail by future philosophers and workers along the lines of psychic research.

NIETZSCHE

Frederick Wilhelm Nietzsche (1844-1900), that brilliant but erratic German philosopher whose extreme and radical conceptions have startled the modern world of thought, flamed into the sky of philosophy like a comet, and disappeared therefrom in like manner. Brilliant to an extreme, he spent his mental energy in running around the circle of thought until he was exhausted, and insanity brought his work to an end. Building upon the foundation of Schopenhauer, and influenced to a degree by von Hartmann, he conceived the idea of a World-Spirit which is ever striving to achieve power in objective manifestation, shape and form, through evolution. He held that "the struggle for existence," and "the survival of the fittest," as taught by the evolutionists, is a cosmic law—and rightly so, for it serves to bring out the strongest and fittest of the manifestations of "The Will," or World-Spirit. He carried the principles of Darwin into the field of ethics and conduct, holding that nature has given us direct teaching upon the subject, and that "might is right," and that it is to the best interest of the race that the strong conquer and persist, and the weak go to the wall and be destroyed. From this struggle and survival, he held, will rise the Over-Man, in whose evolution man is but an instrument and a step. He denounces Christian morality as the "morality of slaves," tending to develop and preserve the weak, and thus interfere with the purposes of the Will. To him the strong is ever the good. But, inconsistent, as are nearly all thinkers, his teaching contains within itself a strong trace of altruism, for does he not teach that we, the race of men, are to model our morals, ethics and lives, upon the idea, and for the purpose of, producing and evolving the Over-Man? By many he is regarded as the prophet of a terrible doctrine of extreme Egoism, but later writers are beginning to see in him but the teacher of a rigid, stern and cruel creed having for its purpose the upbuilding of a strong and powerful race or species of Over-Men. His elemental cruelty and lack of sympathy has made his teaching very repellent to those who are in sympathy with the humanitarian spirit of the age. By such his teaching is regarded as monstrous. But, to others, he seems to have but over-emphasized one phase of the evolutionary urge.

SHAW

To many, the mention of the name of George Bernard Shaw (1856-—) in a list of modern philosophers, may seem strange, so accustomed are the majority of persons to think of this erratic genius as a playwright, essayist, critic, and sociologist. But Bernard Shaw has a philosophy which he subtly introduces in his writings without specifically claiming it to be such. His idea of a fundamental something is expressed by his term "The Life Forces," which he considers as manifesting very much in the same way as does Schopenhauer's "Will to Live," von Hartmann's "Unconscious," or Bergson's "Life Principle." He does not tell us just what the Life Forces are "in themselves," or "in itself," in fact, he at times seems to express the idea that they cannot be known abstractly or independent from objective manifestation. But, at any rate, his Life Forces seem to be seeking along the lines of evolution for higher and more fitter forms of expression, testing and trying first this path, and then that one, often finding themselves in a blind-alley or *cul-de-sac,* and then retreating therefrom only to try another path. Shaw has even intimated that in man the life forces may have run up a *cul-de-sac,* and may be compelled to beat a retreat after a time. Like Nietzsche, Bernard Shaw has a dream of a future greater-man, which he calls the super-man, toward the production of whom the life forces are striving.

BERGSON

Henri Bergson, the French philosopher and author of the recent work entitled "L'Evolution Creatrice" (Creative Evolution) is one of the latest stars noted in the philosophical firmament. A recent English critic has said of his latest work that, "than its entrance upon the field as a well-armed and militant philosophy, there have been not many more memorable occurrences in the world of ideas." Another authority says: "The influence of Bergson is a distinct feature of a new interest in philosophy of which there is abundant evidence in every country. The enthusiasm he has gathered around him is due in the first place to the originality of his speculation, and in the second place, and in a much greater degree, to the promise it offers of raising philosophy to a position in regard to human life and knowledge which has never yet been accorded to it." Whether or not this enthusiastic praise is warranted by the facts must be decided during the next few years when Bergson's philosophy is "tried out" by the fire of criticism to which it will be subjected.

This philosophy has been called "the new idealism," but it is something more (or perhaps less) than this. He describes ultimate reality as being in the nature of a psychical life principle. He holds the reality is the principle of life, itself—not an absolute afar off, but a living something, near to and within us. The intellect is merely a phenomenon of this life principle. The following quotation from H. Wildon Carr, in the "Hibbert Journal," will give a clear, thorough, brief, general idea of Bergson's conception of the life principle:

"Reality is a flux. . . . Life is creative Evolution. Evolution, as we study it in the records of the history that it has left and in the variety of modes in which it has manifested, appears as a succession of forms. Types and species seem to endure for a time and then to give place to other types and species. But there is not real halting; evolution is a continuous change. Life is not static—something now that once was something different—a past left behind and a future spread out in front; it is a single continuous movement, carrying all its past with it and pressing forward into a future which it is forever creating. Evolution is the original impetus of life—the living act in progress. It manifests itself in ever-varying circumstances. The various powers of living beings are the means by which the life activity advances. Of these powers two are especially notable—instinct and intelligence. The former has reached its highest perfection along the line of the invertebrata, especially in ants and bees, and the latter has reached its highest perfection in man. . . . In Bergson's view the intellect is a nucleus formed by a contraction or narrowing of the power of consciousness, and around it is a fringe of more comprehensive consciousness. It is in the possession of this fringe that our power of intuition lies. The intellect has been constructed by the life movement to serve the practical purpose of directing the activities of the living beings possessed of it. Its practical usefulness is due to its limitations. . . . So far as knowledge is concerned, there is insistence that the intellect is neither supreme, nor absolute, nor the only form of knowledge. Intuition is not comparable with the intellect as regards the nature and extent of the knowledge that it puts at our command. Our practical knowledge is entirely intellectual.

But, nevertheless, intuition is a fact, and we have positive evidence of it in ourselves. And a study of other modes of animal existence seems to show that it exists as the normal faculty of knowledge in instinct. Unfortunately from the point of view of pure theory, it is a kind of knowing that, however perfect in its exercise, is apparently limited in its scope. 'There are things that intelligence alone is able to seek, but that by itself it will never find. Those things, instinct alone could find; but it will never seek them.'"

THE PRESENT TENDENCY

Thus we see the present tendency is toward the conception of a world-spirit, or living universe, constantly manifesting itself in forms, shapes and forces. Under the various names used by the later philosophers we may always find this fundamental conception. At the base of all these conceptions is to be found that which may as well be called "spirit" as by any other term.

Voluntarism, in modified forms, is exerting a strong influence in certain quarters of modern philosophical thought and in general literature. It is especially attractive to those who have graduated from materialism, but who find no sympathy for rationalistic idealism. It will probably play an important part in the philosophy of the present century, probably as the active opponent of the schools of rationalistic idealism, just as Schopenhauer was the active opponent of Hegel, the founder of the school of absolute idealism. Supplant the word "Will" by the term "Spirit" and attach the latter to Schopenhauer's philosophy, and we have an agreement with several schools of "advanced thought" metaphysics of to-day, also with Fechner's animistic-pantheism, and Wundt's conception of the universe as the outer wrapper or sheath "behind which is hidden a spiritual creative activity, a striving, feeling, sensing, like that which we experience in ourselves," the active principle of which is conation or impulse, tendency, desire and will.

MATERIALISM

One of the most striking incidents of the history of philosophy is that of the rapid rise into popularity of the doctrine of Materialism in the middle of the nineteenth century. This probably came as a reaction from the extreme emphasis upon Idealism manifested by the German philosophers during the previous century. Moleschott, Vogt and Buchner were the leaders of this school. Their fundamental doctrine was that *the facts of the universe were sufficiently explained by the assumption that matter was the fundamental constituent, or ultimate fact, of the universe, and that all phenomena, including that of consciousness, could be reduced to the transformation of material molecules.* Matter was conceived of as extended, impenetrable, eternally existent, and susceptible of change of relative position. For a few decades radical Materialism flourished, but has since given way to other conceptions.

Agnosticism has largely succeeded it, and, in fact, the former school is often identified in the popular mind with Materialism, although it differs materially from that school.

AGNOSTICISM

Agnosticism, which sprang into favor during the latter half of the nineteenth century, has for its fundamental doctrine the idea that *it is impossible for the human mind to acquire knowledge about God or the Absolute, or, in fact, of anything transcending experience.* Herbert Spencer and Huxley were the leaders in the modern agnostic movement. It has become popular because it easily fits in with the investigations of modern science and the speculations arising therefrom. While both Huxley and Spencer recognize the co-equal reality of mind and matter, their emphasis of the material side has caused many to identify their philosophy with Materialism, which belief is unwarranted. Spencer's position that reality, in itself, is unknowable, and that all things are manifestations of "that infinite and eternal energy from which all things proceed, and which transcends both our reason and our imagination," gives a clear idea of the fundamental position of modern agnosticism.

SCIENTIFIC MONISM

While, as an authority says: "Materialism as a

dogmatic system hardly survives in philosophical circles, although, in alliance with secularism and socialism, it is no doubt influential among certain sections and classes, and often forms the creed of the half-educated specialist. The place of materialism has been taken by scientific Monism, which, however, in some of its representatives, seems often to be but slightly differentiated from the materialism which it has superseded. Scientific Monism is the doctrine that the universe is the manifestation of a single principle of nature. Ernest Haeckel, the German scientist, is the leading exponent of modern "scientific monism." He holds that the fundamental reality consists of a principle of substance, of which matter and force are two aspects, *and in which mind is immanent, and manifest in varying degrees from the atom to man.* He also holds that the entire universe of matter is instinct with life, but inasmuch as he denies immortality and identifies the soul with material form, by some he is classed as an extreme materialist. By many, however, his system is thought likely to evolve into a conception in which materialism and idealism may meet on common ground. In fact, in one of his latest lectures Haeckel admits that his principle of substance may as well be known as "spirit" as by any other term. This admission is wonderfully significant to close students of his philosophy.

POSITIVISM VS. IDEALISM

The rapid development of scientific thought and investigation—the new conceptions of matter and force—the theory of evolution—and the thought that has evolved from these sources, has tended to give to modern philosophy a decided trend toward Positivism, or the doctrine which holds *that philosophical thought must be limited to the data and methods of the natural sciences.* This doctrine is diametrically opposed to the methods of metaphysics, which is now manifesting its fullest flower in Monistic Idealism. And in these two opposing schools we find the secret of the present-day conflict in modern thought. On one side is the extreme "All-Mind" doctrine, and on the other the spirit of natural science, each striving to carry off the prize of philosophy. The struggle is now on, and the dust of the battle somewhat obscures our sight. But through it all I think I see the approaching figure of a mediator who will show the combatants that they are not enemies, but really are brothers-in-arms.

CHAPTER X

THE BUBBLING OF THE POT

In our last chapter I spoke of the Renaissance—that remarkable period of transition from the thought of the Middle Ages to that of modern times—that strange reawakening of religious and philosophical thought, and of art, letters and material progress. The term *renaissance* means, literally, "new birth," and while generally used in the sense of a revival of anything long extinct, lost or obsolete, it has an inner sense or meaning, i. e., the generation of the new individual or thing from the body of the old—the birth of the new generation of the thing. And the Renaissance of the fifteenth and sixteenth centuries affords an excellent illustration of this birth of a new generation of thought. This wonderful period of history manifested "re-birth" of nearly all forms and phases of thought. In philosophy it brought about the death of Scholasticism and the birth of the newer conceptions of reasoning and the tendency to go "back to nature" for truth. In metaphysics it brought about the overturning of the popular Aristotelian thought, and the revival of the Platonic influence under the form of Neo-Platonism. In religion it brought about the attack upon the absolute power and authority of the Church, which resulted in the Reformation and rise of Protestantism. In short, the Renaissance was a period of the sweeping away of old things and the replacing of them with new ideas, new forms, new names. The old, dying, gave birth to the new.

In considering the influences at work to-day in the field of theological, metaphysical, and philosophical thought, one must be struck with their general resemblance to the influences operative during the period of the Renaissance. The same spirit of unrest and the desire for change is manifest. The same iconoclastic tendency on the one hand, and the creative impulse on the other, are seen in to-day's field of thought. The same demand for a new synthesis is heard from the schools of theology, philosophy and metaphysics. The same revival of the search for truth, the same demand for, and willingness to accept truth in whatever form it may present itself, just so it really is truth—and last, the same remarkable revival of interest in the Neo-Platonic philosophy—all these are manifested to-day as strongly as they were in the Renaissance of the fifteenth and sixteenth centuries. In fact, many careful thinkers have expressed the idea that we are now entering into the stage of a new Renaissance—the new generation of thought—the Renaissance of the twentieth century.

And it is this tossing of all the old conceptions

and thought into the great Crucible of Modern Thought—the melting process now under way—and the new Something which is to result therefrom—that forms the subject of this book. We have seen herein the evidences of the great mental and spiritual unrest. We have seen the direct influence of Transcendentalism upon this unrest. We have also traced back to ancient Greece and ancient India the beginning of the ideas observable in the latter-day conceptions. We have re-traced the path of these ideas from the past to the present, showing their influence upon the present thought. We have had, in short, presented to us the various elements and ingredients which have been tossed into the great melting pot of thought. And now, before we venture to prophesy what the outcome is likely to be, let us consider the evidences of the bubbling of the pot—let us see what is being brought to the surface of the pot by the ebullition of the various ingredients under the heat of the fire of mental evolution. For, be it remembered, this is not as yet the period of the new crystallization. We have not as yet reached the period of the new which is to succeed the old. We are merely in the transition stage—the stage of the bubbling pot. The periods of "pouring out," and "cooling," must follow later. Let us now examine the bubbling pot and see what is being brought to the surface.

In the field of theology and religion we are brought

face to face with evidences of the most marked and radical changes. Thoughts which twenty-five years ago would have stamped the utterer thereof as a "free-thinker" are to-day calmly stated without protest from many orthodox pulpits. An examination of the heresy trials of twenty years ago will show that ministers were expelled from their churches for utterances which would pass unnoticed and unrebuked to-day. Thomas Paine, for a century proclaimed as a "heathen," and by an eminent personage called "a dirty little atheist," is seen today to have been not an atheist at all, but merely a Unitarian born a century before his time. Were he living to-day, he would be received in full membership in many of the liberal churches, and his much decried statements would be seen to be practically in accord with many of the findings of the Higher Criticism of the Church of to-day. The universities of to-day are giving utterance to the most heterodox ideas and statements, and yet only here and there an ultra-orthodox clergyman objects.

The Christianity of to-day is an entirely different conception from that of the Christianity of our fathers. There is everywhere among educated people seen the desire to examine the fundamental basis of the theology and doctrine of the Church, and much that was formerly accepted without question is now being thrown overboard by the churches as unwarranted and irrational. The Old Testament conceptions are rapidly losing favor, and Christianity is growing more and more away from the doctrines based thereon. Christianity to-day is adhering closer than ever to the New Testament conceptions—and to the spirit thereof rather than to the letter. It is clinging closer to the Christ ideal than to the Church doctrine, the latter being now regarded as due more to the influence of Paul than to that of his Master. Christianity means a great deal less to many than it did formerly—*but also a great deal more.* It is not too much to say that, while theological Christianity may be declining, the idea and ideals of the Christ are gaining in favor. The theology of the Christian Church is suffering, but the *religion* of Christ is gaining strength, in new forms and from new sources.

Science and Religion, so long thought to be inveterate foes, are now seen to be growing closer together, as new points of agreement are being reached. Science, throwing away much of its former materialistic dogma, and Religion throwing away much of her old theological dogma, find that they are kinspeople and not enemies. It was the old clothing of each which hid the familiar form, and deceived each other and the onlookers. We hear much now of the "Religion of Science" and of the "Science of Religion"—surely a hopeful sign. Religion is now taking into consideration the problems, ideas, conceptions and discoveries of Science, applying them to the religious concepts, the result being the broadening and vitalizing of both. In the more advanced pulpits we hear ministers considering the most radical conceptions of Science, not necessarily to oppose them, but rather endeavoring to blend them with the truths of religion. Both Science and Religion are now seen striving, hand in hand, to discover truth. The best in each camp care nothing as to which side shall make the discovery first—the only concern being that it must and shall be truth. It is true that there are the ultra-orthodox in both camps. There are scientists who hold that "Religion is a huge aberration of the human mind;" and theologians who hold that "Science is atheistic—the handiwork of the Devil." But the most advanced in each camp see the coming of the reconciliation. A writer of a recent scientific book upon "God," when told by a friend that "People will say that the book is written by an atheist," replied: "I would make no objection if they only modify the statement by saying, '*Written by an atheist who loves God.*' "

Dr. Paul Carus, editor of *The Monist,* says: "The best evidence that the scientific spirit pervades the atmosphere of the present age can be seen in the influence which science exercises on religion. There it appears as Biblical Research (sometimes called Higher Criticism); in the study of the history of

Christianity and of other faiths; and in a philosophical purification and deepening of the God-idea."

The same writer characterizes the Monistic position by the following motto:

> "No agnosticism but positive Science,
> Not mysticism but clear thought,
> Neither supernaturalism nor materialism.
> But a unitary conception of the world;
> Not dogma but Religion,
> Not creed but faith."

Passing from the field of theology and religion to that of metaphysics, we find changes equally revolutionary. From being considered the foggiest, most impractical, dreamiest form of speculative thought, we find metaphysics invading the field of the practical and workable. The new metaphysics, arising in response to the spirit of the age, is meeting the requirements of Pragmatism—the test question of which is: "What is it good for? How will it work? What can be done with it? Will it work out in everyday life?" Strange as it may appear to those familiar only with the old conception of metaphysics, the modern demand is for a new metaphysics—a system of metaphysics that may be used in everyday life, and that will be of "some good" to those who may master its principles. This tendency is deplored by those of the old school who hold that the subject of metaphysics must necessarily be entirely removed from that of the phenomenal world and the activities of life, but, be that as it may, it is unquestionably the fact that the trend of the latest metaphysical thought is in the direction of a practical metaphysics and away from the foggy speculations of the past. The material of the past, however, is being used in constructing the new metaphysics. No longer concerned with the abstractions regarding the probable nature of an Absolute which by reason of its very being must be without qualities, attributes or properties, the latter-day metaphysician is inquiring how the underlying something manifests through the individual, and how the individual may avail himself of the cosmic forces behind and in him. The many are asking how the One may be manifested through them. As crude and naive as may be some of these efforts, nevertheless, this is the metaphysical problem of to-day—this is the quality demanded of the new metaphysics.

Passing from the realm of metaphysics into that of philosophy, we find startling changes. The philosophy of to-day, instead of being merely an extension of metaphysical inquiry, has taken on quite a scientific spirit. The inductive method of reasoning has supplanted the deductive in philosophy—the "scientific method" is now the rule. No longer content with the attempt to explain the universe by an assumed principle, philosophy now begins with the universe and strives to work backward to its underlying principles. The "guesses" of the majority of the old philosophers are now regarded merely as the curiosities of philosophical thought. While many of the old thoughts appear in the new systems, they are used in connection with new methods of inquiry. Biology and psychology are blended into the philosophies of to-day—and philosophical theories must square with these branches of science in order to be accepted by thinkers. The old school philosopher evolved a theory of the universe from his own "inner consciousness" and then attempted to explain the universe by means of his theory. If the facts did not agree with or fit in with his theory, well, then "so much the worse for the facts." The new school of philosophers, on the contrary, have made of philosophy a science; indeed, as Dr. Carus has claimed, philosophy is "the science of sciences." This writer speaks as follows regarding the method of scientific inquiry demanded, and observed, in the work of the modern philosopher:

"Science is based upon observation and experience. It starts with describing the facts of our experience, and complements experience with experiment. It singles out the essential features of facts, and generalizes the result in formulas for application to future experience; partly in order to predict coming events; partly, to bring about desirable results. Generalized statements of facts are called truths, and our stock of truths, knowledge. There are always two factors needed for establishing scientific truth, indeed, for establishing any kind of knowledge; they are, first, sense experience, and, second, method. By method we mean the function of handling the material furnished by sense activity, viz., identifying samenesses and differences, comparing various phenomena, i. e., classifying and contrasting them; measuring and counting them; tracing the succession of cause and effect, and arranging the truths thus established into an harmonious whole. . . . The old philosophies are constructions of purely subjective significance, while agnosticism, tired of these vain efforts and lacking strength to furnish a better solution of the problem, claims that the main tasks of philosophy cannot be accomplished; but, if science exists, there ought to be also a philosophy of science, for there must be a reason for the reliability of knowledge. . . . We may confidently hope that the future which the present generation is preparing will be the age of science. . . . Here we have the test of progress. Progress is not, as Spencer says, 'a passage from the homogeneous to a heterogeneous state,' it is the realization of truth. Progress means the growth of soul, and growth of soul means growth of truth. The more clearly, correctly and completely truth is mirrored in a man, the higher he ranges in the scale of evolution."

While modern philosophical thought covers a wide range of speculation and inquiry, and embraces within itself a great variety of conceptions and interpretations, nevertheless it may be safely asserted that it is in its essence Monistic. On all sides we see the disposition to attribute a "Oneness" to the things of the universe—a tendency toward resolving everything back to a one fundamental something. Monism is undoubtedly the prevailing conception of modern philosophical thought. The disputes still rage fiercely over the question of what that one something is, but it is the exception for any leading thinker to question the inherent oneness of things. We have boldly seized the underlying conceptions of the Vedanta, of the Greek philosophers, of Spinoza, and others, and now positively assert in the words of the Hindu thinkers of several thousand years back: "That which *is*, is One—men call it by many names." All, from the most radical Idealist to the most crass Materialist. join in the refrain: "All is One, at the last."

Professor Pringle-Pattison says of Monism:

"Monism is, in strictness, a name applicable to any system of thought which sees in the universe the manifestation or working of a single principle. Such a unity may be said to be at once the tacit pre-supposition and the goal of all philosophic effort, and in so far as a philosophy fails to harmonize the apparently independent and even conflicting facts of experience, as aspects or elements within a larger whole, it must be held to fall short of the necessary ideal of thought. Dualism, in an ultimate metaphysical reference, is a confession of the failure of philosophy to achieve its proper task; and this is the justification of those who consistently use the word as a term of reproach."

The Monism of to-day includes such widely separated schools of thought as those who claim that all is a manifestation of the one principle of Spirit; those who advocate a Higher Pantheism in which all is held to be a manifestation of, and in, God; those who assert that there is but One, and that One is Matter; and those who, like Haeckel, may be considered as scientific Monists, and who hold that the One is substance, possessing the attributes of extension (matter), motion (energy), and conscious (mind). Thus to-day we witness the strange spectacle of the newest new, standing armed with the facts of modern science, biology, psychology, and physics—discarding the subjective philosophies of the intervening period, and looking directly into the eyes of the oldest old which found the conception of the One somewhere in that part of its mind which assures it of the existence of time, space, and causation. The new is ready to "start all over again" just where the old began, but this time basing its advance on scientific research and reasoning, instead of upon mere subjective speculation and theorizing, or "innate truths."

There is one factor, however, which is especially characteristic of the age—the idea of meliorism. Meliorism is "a belief in the possibility of the improvement of the world by human effort, generally implying the further belief that such progressive improvement is a fact and even a law of evolution." Meliorism is the "happy mean" between radical optimism and radical pessimism—between the idea that all that is, is good, and that which holds that all that is, is bad. Sully defines it as: "The faith which affirms not merely our power of lessening evil—this nobody questions—but also our ability to increase the amount of positive good. By recognizing the possibility of happiness and the ability of each individual to do something to increase the sum total of human welfare present and future, meliorism gives us a practical creed sufficient to inspire ardent and prolonged endeavor." Fraser says: "Faith in a gradual abatement of evil by the method of progressive evolution is now a favorite scientific faith;

this faith may be regarded as the form which an unconsciously religious conception of the universe is assuming in professedly agnostic minds." Carus says of this spirit: "The new world-conception, animated by the spirit of science, shows itself in the changes that are wrought not only in our views of the importance of science, but also in practical affairs, in the nature and administration of justice, in the education of children, in our judgment concerning social as well as international affairs, in the way we consider the occurrence of great disasters, such as earthquakes or volcanic eruptions, and in many other things. The spirit of the Middle Ages, with its penal code of barbaric punishments, its cruelty in pedagogy, its narrowness in nationalism and religion, retreats step by step, while truer and broader views that are being more and more universally recognized, herald the advent of an age of science."

As a straw showing which way the philosophical and metaphysical wind is blowing in this first decade of the twentieth century, and as an instance of the recognition of the situation by the orthodox authorities, I call your attention to the following quotation from the leading editorial appearing in *The Interior*, of Chicago, in its issue of August 26, 1909. Coming as this does from the editorial pages of this well-known religious journal, the statement is of remarkable interest to those who are familiar with the modern trend of thought, and particularly in its evident tendency toward the old pantheistic conceptions. The editorial says:

WHAT PREJUDICES MODERN PHILOSOPHY AGAINST A PERSONAL GOD.

"Contemporary philosophers generally assume that it has become impossible in the present age to think of God as a person. Nobody nowadays is an atheist; everybody insists that he believes in God. But if he has aspirations to be recognized as of the guild of the philosophers, he hastens to add that though he believes in God, he does not believe in a God. He conceives God as impersonal—the great Cause pervading the universe.

"Should anyone in the face of this persist in teaching that God is an individual being, with faculties of consciousness, emotion and will, these philosophers by that token rate him no thinker.

"Plain men naturally wonder what it is that the philosophers have found out new to make them so sure God is not individual.

"This answer may not be philosophic, but it is believed fair:

"The present swing to pantheism is not because thinkers have discovered any new facts or developed any new logic which makes personality in God incredible, but because the doctrine of monism is the prevailing creed in metaphysics to-day and pantheism goes easily with that.

"But answering after this fashion manifestly throws back the inquirer to another question—why do modern philosophers so unanimously take to monism?—and that answer is not easy.

"The monist, of course, says he believes in monism because it is true—that nothing else rationally explains existence. And the modern monist is as dogmatic about it as ever the old-time Calvinist was about his five-pointed creed; when you hear the withering scorn with which he speaks of 'the exploded dualistic conception of the universe,' you feel that they must have been poor fools indeed who ever ventured to hold that idea.

"The fact is, however, that the issues at stake between monistic philosophy and opposing propositions are questions that men have been thinking of ever since they thought at all about the kind of world they were living in; and the pendulum of speculation has first swung toward the monistic idea and then away from it, leaving the puzzle of it all still unsettled.

"And although it seems brash to say it in the face of practically all the metaphysicians of the time, even one who knows he is very much of a non-metaphysician may venture the opinion that the present ascendancy of monism is just another swing of the pendulum, which settles nothing, but is presently to be succeeded by an opposite aspect of philosophy.

"At least, the appearance of Professor William James as a pluralist suggests that monism is not just sure of permanence.

"The doctrine of monism is that all the universe is just one thing—one reality—one substance—and that all the different things men see are merely phenomena of the one universal thing. Whence it is easy to proceed to calling that one thing God—which is pantheism.

"Monism doesn't have to teach divine impersonality, however, for if a monist holds that the one unifying reality which composes the universe is Mind, then it is at least philosophically possible to conceive that Mind as possessing consciousness, reason, purpose, love and all the other attributes of personality.

"But the general fact is, that if monism does not require an impersonal Deity necessarily, it arrives there very readily indeed.

"As long, therefore, as monism persists, the plain man need not be surprised to hear a great deal of pantheistic talk among those to whom metaphysics is a more vivid subject than life."

The writer of the above editorial is right when he gives to the general scientific philosophical thought the credit for having turned men's minds in the direction of monism, the doctrine of which he correctly states as, "that all of the universe is just one thing—one reality—one substance—and that all the different things men see are merely phenomena of the one universal thing." But is he likewise right in his conclusion that when that conception is once held in the mind, "it is at least philosophically possible to conceive that mind as possessing consciousness, reason, purpose, *love, and all the other attri-*

butes of personality''? Is there not a vast difference between an absolute principle and a relative personality?

Another straw is seen in the popularity of poems bringing out the idea of the Oneness of All, as, for instance, the following:

ILLUSION

BY ELLA WHEELER WILCOX

God and I in space alone,
And nobody else in view.
And "Where are the people, O Lord," I said,
"The earth below and the sky o'erhead,
And the dead whom once I knew?"

"That was a dream," God smiled and said;
"A dream that seemed to be true;
There were no people living or dead,
There was no earth and no sky o'erhead,
There was only Myself and you."

"Why do I feel no fear," I asked,
"Meeting YOU here in this way?
For I have sinned, I know full well;
And is there heaven, and is there hell,
And is this the judgment day?"

"Nay! those were dreams," the great God said,
"Dreams that have ceased to be;
There is no such thing as fear, or sin;
There is no YOU—you never have been—
There is nothing at all but ME!"

When such verse as this—verse which utters sentiments, and expresses ideas, as radical and as advanced in line of Absolute Idealism as any philosophical concept mentioned in this book, not excepting the Vedantic idea—then are we not warranted in believing that the wind is blowing strongly from a certain quarter of the world of thought—are we not warranted in calling attention to the fact that the pot is bubbling very fiercely and that certain ingredients are appearing very frequently and forcibly upon the surface of the seething compound; and in believing that when the material is finally poured forth, and exposed after cooling, then the new thing will be strongly colored with Pantheistic Idealism?

CHAPTER XI

NEW THOUGHT, THEOSOPHY AND CHRISTIAN SCIENCE

And now we are brought to a consideration of a phase of modern thought which has attracted much attention from observers of the "signs of the times." This phase combines within itself the elements of religion, metaphysics and philosophy, although the orthodox authorities in each of these fields of thought will likely insist that the words "*quasi*" or "*pseudo*" be placed before each of these respective terms when so used. We allude to that peculiar manifestation of the modern mental and spiritual unrest which, under its manifold forms and names, may be generally termed the "New Thought." It is true that we group under this heading several schools and sects which indignantly repudiate that particular term, but, nevertheless, we believe that the said term may be properly applied to all of this class of thought for the purpose of general classification, leaving the various elements to fight out for themselves which of them are orthodox and which otherwise. No other term applies so well to this particular manifestation of modern thought and speculation. It combines within itself the elements of many phases of theology, religion, metaphysics and philosophy, and yet is different from any and all of them. That is, the peculiar combination and application is different. "New Thought" is *sui generis*—unique—of its own kind. *"In itself" it is incapable of definition—it is known only through its various manifestations.*

In the first place, "New Thought" is *new* only in its present combination—its respective elements are as old as religious, metaphysical and philosophical thought. It represents a new turn of the kaleidoscope of speculation—the old elements are merely grouped in new form. Perhaps this idea may best be described by the apropos, although somewhat flippant, verses hereto appended, which have been going the round of the newspapers and magazines, including several devoted to the subject of "New Thought" itself. The author, whose name is unknown to me, breaks into descriptive verse as follows:

"Take a page of Epictetus and a Plato paragraph;
Shake it briskly till the mixture makes the gentle scoffers chaff.
Add a slight Socratic flavor, not in excess of a dram,
And a weak solution formed of Persian epigram.
Mix a bit from old Confucius and from Buddha several drops,
Add Egyptian lore found in the pyramid of great Cheops.
Now some truths not half remembered and some others half forgot.
Boil the mixture, boil it briskly, till it simmers in the pot;
And—Lord bless you now, my brother, and the skeptics all beshrew—
Can't you see that you're approaching the thought that's labeled 'New?'

. . . .

'It is Thought,' I said with rev'rence, much of which is very true,
But, if I do not displease you, what in thunder makes it New?'

Came the answer, 'Lo! poor skeptic, hear the truth and doubt no more;
Such a mixture's mixful mixing never has been mixed before.' "

Perhaps we may get a clearer idea of the nature of the "New Thought" if we will consider two of its leading direct sources, both of which, by the way, indignantly disclaim all relationship with, and inclusion in, the "New Thought." These two direct sources, through which has flowed the older waters of many ancient schools of thought are, respectively, "Theosophy" and "Christian Science."

"Theosophy," in the modern application of the term, was a school of thought founded in 1875 by Helena Petrovna Blavatsky, the theories and teachings of which were promulgated by the Theosophical Society founded at that time. The Society has since had a varied experience, with several schisms and separations. Its teachings, however, have spread so far beyond its own organization that, today, "Theosophy" is regarded more as a general teaching than as the particular belief of the Society, or of its divided schools. The sources of the Theosophical doctrine are various, principal among which, however, are the teachings of the ancient Greek Mystics and the Buddhists, these two being ingeniously blended and commingled in the fundamental beliefs of the cult. The following "three fundamental propositions" of Theosophy are gleaned from the writings of the founder:

I. An omnipresent, eternal, boundless and immutable principle on which all speculation is impossible, since it transcends the power of human conception and could only be dwarfed by any human expression or similitude.

II. The eternity of the universe in toto as a boundless plane, periodically the playground of numberless universes incessantly manifesting and disappearing.

III. The fundamental identity of all souls with the universal OverSoul, the latter being itself an aspect of the unknown root; and the obligatory pilgrimage of every soul—a part of the OverSoul—through the cycle of incarnation in accordance with cyclic and karmic law, during the whole term. No privileges or special gifts are possessed by man save those won by his own Ego through personal effort and merit throughout a long series of reincarnations.

Upon this superstructure a great edifice of dogma and speculation has been built. Theosophy explains everything in the heavens above, the earth beneath, and the waters under the earth—to the satisfaction of its followers—all worked out in detail, and capable of diagraming and blackboard demonstration. Prominent in its teachings we find the detailed theories regarding clairvoyance, telepathy, second-sight, spirit-return, astral bodies, etc., and particularly the favorite New Thought doctrine that "thoughts are things," and that it is possible to influence another by one's projected thoughts, even though great distances intervene. The earlier Theosophical books, as well as the later, have many references to this power of thought, and the "New Thought" undoubtedly received many of its ideas on this subject, directly and indirectly, through Theosophy. Prentice Mulford, a writer of the early '80's, did much to popularize Theosophical ideas and conceptions, and was a direct connecting link between Theosophy and the "New Thought," his favorite axiom: "Thoughts are Things," having become quite a slogan of the latter. The Theosophical doctrine of reincarnation and Karma have found much favor among many of the followers of "New Thought," although others reject it and favor the idea of a spiritual progression from plane to plane, higher and higher, toward the one divine principle. Its pantheistic ideas are also very apparent in many of the several cults of the "New Thought" movement. It must be noted, however, that Theosophy has had but little to say regarding "healing" of physical ills by mental and spiritual power—so the "New Thought" is not under obligations to it for this part of the latter's working creed, this feature having been derived from other sources.

"Christian Science," the most successful of any of the cults which are grouped under the general term of "New Thought," was founded by Mary

Baker Eddy in the '60's, although it did not rise into popular favor for many years after that time. Whether or not Mrs. Eddy received her inspiration from Dr. P. P. Quimby, as some claim, is outside the matter of the present consideration. Whatever may have been the history of her start in the movement, the fact is indisputable that the "Christian Science" of to-day is the result of her own energy, ability and judgment, and she is justly entitled to her claim of "founder" and actual promoter of the movement. Without Mrs. Eddy, "Christian Science" would not be known as it is to-day.

The Christian Scientists hold that no one not a member of their organization can have sufficient knowledge of its principles to explain them, or even intelligently discuss them. This may be so, and the best I can do is to present for your consideration the fundamental principles of Christian Science *as they seem to be* upon careful inquiry.

It would seem that Christian Science is based upon the fundamental idea of the existence of an omnipresent, omnipotent, and omniscient principle of Being, known as "God," the divine individuality of which (or whom) can be discerned only spiritually and supersensibly, and which cannot be cognized by "mortal mind" or the so-called material senses. God is held to be Life, Truth, Love, Spirit and the Divine Principle of all true Being, and the sole creative principle, cause, origin, source, basis, foundation, government, and law of all that has actual and permanent existence. God is also held to be the sole Substance—that is, that the Divine Spirit-Mind is the only actual, immortal substance or reality. *The Divine Mind is held to be conscious only of good, spirit, life and health,* and does not create *or consent to* any form of evil, sin, sickness, death, or matter, which, instead, are held to be "errors of mortal mind"—abnormalities and monstrosities—the negation of Truth—"the paraphernalia of an ignorant and depraved sense of existence which are but relative qualities, and both of which fear, sin, superstition, ignorance, and an erroneous philosophy—"mortal mind," in short—are held to constitute the primal cause of the degradation which has involved the human race in mortality, which, however, is, may be, and will be, overcome by the knowledge of the Truth which is in Christian Science.

It will be seen at once, by those who have followed us in the preceding chapters, that the fundamental principle of Christian Science is essentially idealistic. It partakes of the nature of the conception of Bishop Berkeley, but in many ways is nearer to the idealism of the centuries-old advanced school of the Vedanta Philosophy of India. Both hold that there is but one reality—one life—one substance—that of the Absolute, or God. Both hold that the material universe is illusory and that all things exist only as ideas in the mind of the One. The Vedantist claims that "the appearance of the phenomenal world, with its succession of change, and its plurality of souls," is due to *maya* (illusion) arising from *avidya* (ignorance) which binds the individual until the scales drop from his eyes and he sees the Truth of the Oneness. The Christian Scientist holds that the material world is non-existent in reality, but arises from "the errors of mortal mind" which may be overcome by a knowledge of the Truth which is in Christian Science. In many particulars Christian Science seems to run "on all fours" with the idealism of the past and present—Oriental and Occidental—but in one important particular it diverges, and this one particular is claimed by its followers to be all-important.

We allude to the fact that Christian Science holds that the Divine Mind actually images and is conscious of only the good, the beautiful and the true, and does not idealize, image, create, form *or consent to* the evil, sin, sickness or death, which are held to be pure illusion or "errors of mortal mind." The Vedanta, and similar philosophies, on the contrary, hold that the Absolute is "above good and evil," which are but relative qualities, and both of which are alike unreal and illusory. Justice requires that this distinction be noted in all comparisons of Christian Science and other forms of Idealism. The origin of "mortal mind" of Christian Science is not explained in its philosophy, although it is stated to have no basis in reality. Like the *maya* and *avidya* of the Hindus it appears to be an illusory cause of illusion—a series of negation of Truth. At the best, both would seem to be the result of circular reasoning. It would seem to the humble observer that an all-wise, all-powerful, all-loving Absolute or Supreme Being, could and *would* prevent the arising of *maya* or "mortal mind," or at least immediately destroy such if it did arise. Unless, indeed, we admit, with Hegel, that the "negation" or "opposite" of everything, even Truth, must exist from the very nature of Truth itself.

The authorities inform us that religion depends upon two elements: (1) The perception of need on the part of the individual; and (2) the belief in the existence of some higher power which can and will relieve the need. When a man turns to some believed-in higher power, and supplicates it, in faith and trust, to help him and to relieve his distress, then and there that man becomes a religious being. Schleirmacher claims that religion is "the feeling of dependence." If this conception be true, then the Christian Scientist becomes the most religious of religious beings, for he depends upon God for everything, at all times. Not content, as is the ordinary churchman, with asking merely for a home in a better land after death, with occasional answers to prayer, the Christian Scientist expects and demands of God the alleviation of every ill; the balm for every pain; health, happiness, and prosperity. In fact, he holds that these things really exist for him in the Divine Mind, and that only the error and illusion of "mortal mind" prevent them from being in constant evidence. It must be confessed that of all the idealistic philosophies, that of Christian Science holds the greatest promise of pragmatic results—the "working out" and "making good" being confidently promised to those who will follow its teachings. It is true that, to the uninitiated, "material good" seems as much allied to the world of materiality as does "material evil"—and as much the result of illusion, *maya*, or "mortal mind." But, then, after all, it is probably true that one must *be* a Christian Scientist in order to fully *understand* its teachings.

Christian Science holds that its healing and removal of error is wholly the result of spiritual power—and arises from the perception of the Truth. It claims to have nothing in connection with suggestion, mental healing, faith-cure, and other forms of healing manifested by the various "New Thought" schools and others—these manifestations being regarded as merely "mortal mind" counterfeits of the real—the serpents of the magicians as compared with the serpent of Moses, and, like the former, destined to be swallowed and destroyed by the Truth. The most dangerous of all forms of "mortal mind" to the Christian Scientist, is that known as "malicious animal magnetism," which is akin to hypnotism, mesmerism, and general evil mental malpractice. This "M. A. M." seems to be the "devil" of Christian Science, although to an outsider it would seem that if the fundamental tenets of the faith be true, there would be no cause for alarm. By many kindly disposed and sympathetic critics of Christian Science this "M. A. M." belief is regarded as an ugly excrescence upon a beautiful philosophy. Let it be hoped that time will remove it.

It is absurd to deny the fact that Christian Science has exerted a most potent influence upon the "New Thought" movement. It is a fact that many of the "New Thought" teachers were originally Christian Scientists, and left the fold chiefly because they resented the authority of Mrs. Eddy, and sought to exercise a greater personal influence of their own. Even among those who did not serve their apprenticeship in "C. S.," there is found a practical adoption of one or more of Mrs. Eddy's principles, varied to suit the particular views of the adapter. "Mental Science," a prominent branch of the "New Thought," adheres to the practical features of Christian Science while using the term "Mind" in place of "God." Other added features have been borrowed from Theosophy and the religions and philosophies of ancient India and Greece. In fact, the philosophies of all countries and times have been drawn upon by "New Thought" until the verse quoted a little further back is almost literally true.

Mental Suggestion, particularly in its form of auto-suggestion, has been boldly borrowed from the New Psychology, and dressed up as "affirmations," "statements," etc. The world-old principles of Faith Healing (really based upon Suggestion) have been used, under various names and guises, and with various explanations and theories. The old ideas of "magic," or mental influence at a distance, have been blended with the Psychic Research theories of telepathy. The theories of the New Psychology (and of Hindu philosophy) regarding the subconscious and superconscious planes of mentality have been worked over into a semi-religious philosophy. Through Dr. Quimby, Dr. Evans, and Julian A. Dresser, the "Quimby" theories have reached "New Thought," but the methods of applying the same are found to have been adapted from Mrs. Eddy's "Science" in the majority of cases. Faith Cure and Mental Healing, however, are as old as the race, and there is no need for a discussion between cults or schools on that point. It is merely a question of names and theories.

I shall not speak at length regarding the successes and failures of the "New Thought" movement. Enough for me to say that "New Thought" contains within itself much of the very highest in human thought, belief, and philosophy, together with much of the lowest and most regrettable superstition, credulity and false-knowledge. In so far as it has manifested truth, the movement has succeeded; in so far as it has manifested superstition, it has failed. It is the belief of some careful observers that the movement will eventually split itself up into three great sections—the first of which will be absorbed by Christian Science; the second, resolving itself into a "Religion of Science" or a "Science of Religion," with a fundamental belief in the Fatherhood of God, the Brotherhood of Man, the Mastery of Self, the development of the powers latent in the mind of man and inherent in all nature; the third, degenerating into a cult or cults of credulous superstition, low forms of psychism and gross forms of occultism, revival of the witchcraft delusion, fetichism, and perhaps even phallicism and "voodooism." For be it remembered, there are dark sides to mysticism and occultism, as well as the bright sides.

The "New Thought" movement is not homogeneous, but is composed of a great variety of cults, schools, and varieties of belief and practice, and but loosely united. In its garden are many choice flowers and many rank and poisonous weeds, the seeds of both having been sown long ago by the thinkers of the past and now being watered by the rain of change and warmed by the sun of interest, have grown and borne flower and fruit, each according to its kind.

From this garden may be expected much, good and evil, which will influence the thought of the future. Its flowers have begun to cross-fertilize each other, and many new varieties will spring up to perplex the philosophers of to-morrow. Surely "such a mixful mixture ne'er has been mixed before," of the seeds of old Egypt, India, Chaldea, Persia, Greece—Hinduism, Buddhism, Paganism, Christianity, Religion, Metaphysics, Philosophy, Rationalism, Mysticism, Occultism. What shall the harvest be?

Added to the other elements bubbling in the pot, and now showing at the surface, we find the great sociological and economic problems manifested by the rise of Socialism, Labor Unionism, Single Tax, and the rest—all of which will exert a strong influence in the new composite material which will presently flow from the pot. Then there must be recognized the inquiry and investigation of the Psychic Researchers, who have lifted Spiritualism to the plane of science. If survival of the individual soul can be scientifically established, it will give a new impetus to thought in that direction, and will extend the domain of science beyond the border. If science can prove the theory of telepathy beyond a doubt, many of the theories regarding life and mind will have to be revised. We are indeed entering into a period of philosophical, metaphysical, theological and sociological rebirth. The New Renaissance is upon us. The pot is bubbling fiercely—strange things are coming to the surface and showing their form. What will eventually flow forth from the pot to cool and crystallize—then to await the coming of another era of the Melting Pot? Ah! what, indeed?

CHAPTER XII

THE DAWN OF TO-MORROW

It may be considered a somewhat presumptuous undertaking to venture upon even a tentative speculation as to what is likely to be crystallized from the Crucible of Modern Thought after the great melting process is over for the time being. But it is difficult to refrain from attempting a prediction based upon the appearance of the molten mass of philosophic thought at the present time. It is true that some new combination may be formed which will give to the thought of the future a now entirely unsuspected shape, but, nevertheless, careful thinkers feel that the general form of the thought of to-morrow may be predicted at the present time with a fair degree of accuracy, if the prophets be sufficiently well acquainted with the influences operative in the thought of to-day.

In the first place there seems to be a strong probability that the thought of to-morrow will be largely Monistic. Under the various speculations of materialism and idealism there is ever to be found the idea of the One Something from which all the universe proceeds. Materialism holds that the universe is, at the first and last, primarily and ultimately, matter or substance conceived of as extended, impenetrable, eternally existent, and susceptible of movement or change of relative position. Idealism holds that the universe is throughout the work or the embodiment of reason or mind. Spencer held in effect that both mind and substance are aspects of a higher and final reality—"that infinite and eternal energy from which all things proceed," and which in its inner nature was unknowable, being of such a nature as to transcend and defy apprehension by any of the processes by which the human mind apprehends its objects. And our prediction is that the thought of to-morrow will hold closely to the conception of Spencer, and will postulate the existence of an ultimate principle, of which the universe is a manifestation, and of which mind and substance are the opposing poles, phases or aspects.

It is impossible to think of mind independent of substantial embodiment, and it is likewise impossible to think of substance without the indwelling mind. Whatever is evolved must first have been involved, and if mind were never involved in substance it can never have been evolved from it. And, likewise, if substance were never involved in mind, it could never have been evolved from it. So, at the last, the dispute between the advocates of universal mind and of universal substance, respectively—the idealists and the materialists—is seen to be merely a question of: "Which is the highest or primary manifestation? Did the phenomenon called matter, antedate and evolve mind, or did the phenomenon called mind antedate and evolve matter?" (S. E. Stevens.) The coming thinker will almost certainly hold that both mind and matter are merely opposite poles, phases, or aspects of the one underlying reality.

I also predict that this one underlying reality will be thought of as Spirit. By "Spirit" I mean the *Essence of the All*, containing within itself both the principle of form, shape and mass which we call substance; and the principle of awareness or consciousness which we call mind. As G. E. Moore says:

> "Common to all meanings of 'spirit' is the conception of that which is conscious. Consciousness itself is not conceived as *being* spirit, but as being an attribute of it; so that spirit is conceived as something capable of existing, even when it is not conscious. On the other hand, there is no positive conception of *what* this permanent element in spirit is; it is only conceived abstractly as *that* (whatever it may be) *which is the substance or subject of consciousness*, and negatively as not identical with any known *quale* (quality)."

This usage of the term "Spirit" must not be confounded with other and more common forms of usage. We can perhaps best think of it in the terms of Spencer, i. e., as "that infinite and eternal energy from which all things proceed." Therefore, I feel that here will be found a reconciliation between the advanced thinkers of the opposing schools of idealism and materialism, the agreement being based upon the common conception of an ultimate reality known as Spirit in which the opposite phenomena of substance and mind meet, blend, and have their origin and end, and of which both mind and substance are but relative aspects, phases, poles, or manifestations. I believe that the close of the twentieth century will find philosophers and scientists both discussing ultimates in terms not of matter nor of mind, but of Spirit. And, I believe that from this common conception a new synthesis will arise, acceptable alike to philosophy, science and religion.

But, I do not follow the idea of Spencer to the extent that I believe that the thought of to-morrow will hold that this ultimate reality—Spirit—is unknowable. On the contrary I believe that evolution will bring forth in man faculties and powers of understanding whereby he will be enabled to know more and more regarding ultimate things which are now classed as transcendental and defying apprehension by the mind of man. I believe that the thought of to-morrow will use the term "unknown" even more frequently than that of to-day, but that the term "unknowable" will be banished. *I believe in the infinite possibility of expansion and evolution of mind.*

As S. E. Stevens says: "We do not know and cannot comprehend; but if it becomes essential for mankind to know—infinite nature will evolve an organ of mind that can comprehend. A part of the infinite, man's possibilities of knowing must be infinite. What has taken ages to evolve a wish to understand, will require ages to develop ability to understand!" As Haeckel has said: "There is no scientific problem which we may dare to say the mind of man will never solve; no mystery so deep or profound; no question ever has or ever will be asked, but a mind or brain will be evolved and developed capable of solving and answering." In fact, even to-day careful thinkers have found signs of the budding of faculties or mental powers which register impressions of things ordinarily called transcendental—which give the report of a consciousness other than that dependent upon the ordinary senses. Of this I shall speak further as we proceed.

The thinker of the end of the twentieth century will label things "known," "unknown," or "to be known," but never "unknowable." He will point to the limits of the "known" and say "here our present knowledge ends," in the true scientific spirit, but he will never commit the folly of saying "Here knowledge ends and the unknowable begins." To the coming thinker physics and metaphysics will be branches of one field of investigation, and that field will be called the *Science of Truth.* I believe that eventually the distinction between physics and metaphysics will be wiped out—that the natural and the supernatural will be seen to be equally phases of the greater nature.

But what of the religion and theology of to-morrow? It is indeed a brave man (or a foolish one) who will attempt to answer this question. But, judging from present indications I think it safe to hazard the speculation that the conception of the immanent and indwelling God will have won the victory over the conceptions of a Deity removed from the universe—who made the universe out of nothing and then set it going like a watch, standing aside to see how it worked. Perhaps the better way to indicate what I believe will be the prevailing religious conception of to-morrow would be to call your attention to the signs of the evolution of that conception to-day. For instance consider the remarkable statement of Prof. Charles W. Eliot, late President of Harvard entitled "The Religion of the Future" as published in the *Harvard Theological Review* of October, 1909, from the report of the lecture delivered July 22, 1909, before the Harvard Summer School of Theology. The reader who is familiar with the prevailing ideas of the New Thought will be struck by the remarkable resemblance to the latter, although Professor Eliot arrived at his conclusion independently. Among other things Professor Eliot said:

"The new thought of God will be its most characteristic element. This ideal will comprehend the Jewish Jehovah, the Christian Universal Father, the modern physicist's omnipresent and exhaustless Energy, and the biological conception of a Vital Force. The Infinite Spirit pervades the universe, just as the spirit of a man pervades his body, and acts, consciously or unconsciously, in every atom of it. The twentieth century will accept literally and implicitly St. Paul's statement, 'In Him we live, and move, and have our being,' and God is that vital atmosphere, or incessant inspiration. The new religion is therefore thoroughly monotheistic, its God being the one infinite force; but this one God is not withdrawn or removed, but indwelling and especially dwelling in every living creature. God is so immanently immanent in all things, animate and inanimate, that no meditation is needed between Him and the least particle of His creation. In His moral attributes, He is for every man the multiplication to infinity of all the noblest, tenderest and most potent qualities which that man has ever seen or imagined in a human being. In this sense every man makes his own picture of God. Every age, barbarous or civilized, happy or unhappy, improving or degenerating, frames its own conception of God within the limits of its own experiences and imaginings. In this sense, too, a humane religion has to wait for a humane generation. The central thought of a new religion will therefore be a humane and worthy idea of God, thoroughly consistent with the nineteenth century revelations concerning man and nature, and with all the tenderest and loveliest teachings which have come down to us from the past.

"The scientific doctrine of one omnipresent, eternal Energy, informing and inspiring the whole creation at every instant of time and throughout the infinite spaces, is fundamentally and completely inconsistent with the dualistic conception which sets spirit over against matter, good over against evil, man's wickedness against God's righteousness, and Satan against Christ. The doctrine of God's immanence is also inconsistent with the conception that He once set the universe a-going, and then withdrew, leaving the universe to be operated under physical laws, which were His vicegerents or substitutes. If God is thoroughly immanent in the entire creation, there can be no 'secondary causes,' in either the material or the spiritual universe. The new religion rejects absolutely the conception that God is alienated from the world. It rejects also the entire conception of man as a fallen being, hopelessly wicked, and tending downward by nature; and it makes this emphatic rejection of long-accepted beliefs because it finds them all inconsistent with a humane, civilized or worthy idea of God."

I am of the opinion that one of the novel features of the religion of To-morrow will be a remarkable blending of the doctrine of empiricism with that of faith. Empiricism holds that all knowledge must be the result of experience; and is usually identified with sensationalism, or the doctrine that all knowledge results from sensations, and that all cognitions, even reflective ideas and so-called intuitions, can be traced back to elementary sensations. This doctrine has always been regarded as diametrically opposed to the theory of innate ideas and of faith. But there has arisen a new school of thinkers who hold that faith itself is based, not upon mere blind belief, but upon *actual experience* of things usually regarded as transcendental and above experience. It is being earnestly urged that man is developing new faculties —*spiritual faculties*—through and by means of which he *may actually experience the spiritual world.* It is held that just as mere sensation was succeeded first by the faculties of feeling, from which in succession evolved the organs and faculties of hearing, taste, smell, and sight, all of which are modifications and improvements upon the original sense of feeling, so in his evolution there is now coming to man the spiritual faculty or sense by means of which he may be able to *know* those things which are now usually regarded as beyond experience and as merely objects of faith. These thinkers hold that there is evolving a new faith which not only *believes,* but actually *knows.* Following this line of thought, it is deemed reasonable to believe that in the course of evolution *Man may grow to actually know God, truth and immortality.*

As significant of this line of thought may be instanced Prof. Wm. James' work entitled *"Varieties of Religious Experience;"* and Dr. Maurice Bucke's work entitled *"Cosmic Consciousness."* In Professor James' work are recited numerous instances, ancient and modern, which indicate the existence in man of certain super-conscious faculties which give to him information and experience regarding the transcendental planes of being, thought, and action. The writer of the work argues for the validity of this class of experiences, and indicates his belief in the idea that the race is evolving higher faculties whereby the spiritual planes of life may be *perceived and known* just as are the things of the material plane. In Dr. Bucke's work is advanced the idea that man is evolving into a new phase of consciousness termed cosmic consciousness, just as he has previously evolved from sensation to simple consciousness, and from simple consciousness into self-consciousness.

Cosmic consciousness is held to be an awareness of the unity of the cosmos; the oneness of all; the living universe; immortality; and other things usually regarded as belonging to the transcendental plane. Among the truths reported by Dr. Bucke as experienced by those to whom flashes of "cosmic consciousness" come, are the following: The seeing and knowing "that the cosmos is not dead matter but a living presence; that the soul of man is immortal; that the universe is so built and ordered that without any peradventure all things work together for the good of each and all; that the foundation principle of the world is what we call love; and that the happiness of everyone is in the long run absolutely certain." It will be seen that there is a growing inclination to attach the seal of validity to the higher mystical and religious experiences of the race, instead of regarding them as merely the result of emotional excitement. I believe that this conception will play an important part in the thought of to-morrow, after the grain of higher spiritual experiences is separated from the chaff of the abnormal "psychic" phenomena.

There is almost a certainty that the thought of to-morrow will recognize the value and efficacy of faith in the affairs of everyday life; and that a basis of reality will be found for the apparently miraculous and wonderful experiences of man in the past and present, such as the answer to prayer, faith cures, and much of the phenomena of New Thought, Christian Science, and similar beliefs. It would seem that the race is acquiring methods of becoming "in tune with the Infinite," and drawing to itself some of the wonderful powers, energies and material from the higher planes of being. It will be seen that the answer to prayer based on faith comes not as a special intervention of a higher being, but rather as the result of the drawing by the individual of the power of the All. The power of faith is dynamic, and, underlying the creeds, beliefs, and theories there is undoubtedly to be found truths regarding the occasional employment of the higher forces of the universe in response to the earnest belief of the individual, no matter upon whom or what this belief is bestowed. It is practically assured that this phenomena will be accepted, investigated and scientifically explained by the thinkers of To-morrow.

It is extremely probable that the problems of Psychic Research will be well threshed out before long; the false discarded and the remnant of truth extracted and used as the basis for further investigation into the "Night-side of Nature." It is safe to hazard the prediction that this investigation will lift the accepted phenomena from the realm of the supernatural, and will place them in their proper position in the kingdom of the natural.

It is perhaps a daring guess to predict that before long telepathy will be much better understood and that communication between mind and mind without the employment of spoken word or sign will be quite common. It would be interesting to speculate what would be the result on the life of the race were telepathy to become a common possession of all persons. If all persons were able to *read* the minds of each other, all pretense, hyprocrisy, fraud, lying, deception and untruth would vanish as the mist before the rising sun. If each could read the truth in the mind of the other, truth would reign and falsehood disappear—the conventional lies of civilization would fade away; the "Ananias Club" would stand forth self-confessed; and the liar would be shunned as pestilential. If the gift of perfect telepathy were to be given the race overnight, the morning would witness the greatest social and moral revolution of all time. If each could gaze into the soul of every other—if the naked soul of each were perceived by all—then each individual would stand forth as in the legendary "Day of Judgment," and men and women would then be graded according to their real worth or unworth, rather than by their pretensions, claims, and false reputation. In that day *Character*, not *Reputation*, would be the real standard. I do not mean to indicate our belief that the men of tomorrow will possess this degree of development, but merely to show the possibilities in connection with the probabilities of the increasing knowledge on this subject.

I think it extremely likely that to-morrow will possess a scientific knowledge of the underlying principles of Mental Suggestion, and the powers of the mind which form the subject of attention of so many schools, cults and writers to-day. I think that the creative imagination and the dynamic will will be accepted as actual constructive forces. I believe that an entirely new field of scientific research will be opened up through an appreciation of these subjects. I think that just as the other natural forces have been raised from the category of superstition and base credulity, and are now mastered and used in the service of the race, so will the great forces of the mind be raised from the category of superstition, pseudo-science, and absurd theories, and, being understood by science, will be used intelligently for the upbuilding of the race.

I feel that many social and economic changes are coming to the race, the advance movement of which has even now begun. But I believe that the real change will come not alone by reason of the dissatisfaction of the masses, and the increasing burden of living under the present economic conditions, but also by reason of the dawning "social conscience" of the race. I believe that this "social conscience" is a forerunner of the cosmic consciousness of which I have spoken. I believe that the evolving sense of the oneness of all life—the dawning awareness that life is one at the last, and that each is a part of that One, and closely related to every other part—will bring about a new sense of the brotherhood of man. Already we may see signs of this dawning consciousness of the race. Men are *beginning to feel the "world pain."* When we feel the pain of our brother, then we will be impelled to relieve his pain. The sympathy which comes from the growing and extending consciousness of the individual, must eventually cause the pain of one to be the pain of all —the joy of one to become the joy of all. With this enlarged consciousness must necessarily come the tearing down of the present cruel conditions which afflict so many of our brothers and sisters, and the building up of a new social and economic structure in which the human family will be felt to include every individual, even the lowest and most unworthy; and with this feeling must come the exertion of every power of the race to raise up the downtrodden and depraved, and to unite all once more at the table of the Father. I predict that in this way will come the "social revolution" that so many have looked for in some other form.

I predict that these and other great and wonderful changes shall and will come to the human thought of to-morrow, and that the active principle operating under and in all these changes will be seen to be that most marvelous of all forces known to man—the Law of Love. Just as the original self-love of the primitive man developed so as to include his mate, and then his offspring; then his family; then his tribe; then his confederation of tribes; then his nation; then all of kindred speech and beliefs; then in constantly broadening circles according to his development—so will the man of to-morrow, feeling the dawning Cosmic Consciousness, learn to love *every living thing,* reaching out extend understanding, sympathy and love to the all in All. For at the last, Love not only "makes the world go round," but is also the cause of every uplift and improvement that the world has ever experienced. Indeed, many careful thinkers believe that in Love we have the explanation of Evolution itself.

William Marion Reedy says:

"Man has always felt that there was nothing inanimate, from the beginning of time. His intuition has always been in advance of his reason. His poetry has led his science everywhere. The Oneness of things is being demonstrated in these days; that is all. . . . God, in every language was both masculine and feminine. Life is but force. Matter holds together by force. Matter therefore has life. . . . The star is brother to the clod; the moth is kin to the mastodon. Worlds are made to blossom in space as flowers are fructified by floating pollen. Mingling atoms make suns. Cell seeks affinity with cell. Dust blown from the unimaginable outer rim of silence finds its fellow dust and a nebula is formed, and from that nebula suns and systems of suns. Worlds in contact give birth to worlds. The crystals meet and kiss and mingle and produce other crystals. . . . Love is the only law. Love is spirit, and matter the child of spirit. All this any man who reads may know. . . . But where does it end—this intelligent Love? There is a limit to the finite. But the finite is part of the Infinite. It would seem that the pursuit of the law of love would bring one only to the unknowable, pushing it only a little further back. Love may follow where love leads—unto the essence of God even—for God is Love. The material aspect of love, dwelt on so far, need not deter us from pushing 'farther North.' To those who believe in the Oneness of Matter and Spirit, there is no unknowable. The end of the law of Love, and of the spiritual faculties for its perception, can be the knowing of this unknowable—union with the Infinite. Let us make a flight."

And this then is my feeble conception of what tomorrow may bring forth. I may have erred in the details, but I feel certain that I have seen and mentioned the general trend of the coming thought. The urge of Evolution, material, mental and spiritual, is still under way. The womb of the future contains unborn good beyond the wildest dreams, hopes and anticipations of man. The very hopes and aspirations of the highest of the race are but prophecies of their ultimate fulfillment and realization. But, after all, the mere intellectual conception of philosophies, metaphysics, theologies, theories of all sorts and kinds are of the *mind* alone—the only satisfying realization is that which comes from *the soul itself*, the message of the spirit. The realization indwelling in the soul of each brings to the troubled mind "that peace which passeth all understanding," and stills the tempest raging within the thought of each individual who dares ask himself "why?" and 'how?" After traveling round and round the endless circle of thought—after running up all the blind-alleys of speculation—rest and peace come only when one regains the Holy of Holies within his soul.

For at the end of our philosophical speculations, how many of us but echo the words of Emerson:

> "I laugh at the love and the pride of man,
> At the sophist schools and the learned clan,
> For what are they all, in their high conceit,
> When man in the bush with God may meet?"

How many a soul perplexed by circular reasoning; fatiguéd by running around the speculative wheel of the squirrel-cage of thought; or bruised by having dashed its wings against the bars of the cage of Experience, in which it has been confined, finds comfort and peace in the words of good old Newman:

"Lead kindly Light, amid the encircling gloom;
Lead thou me on,
The night is dark, and I am far from home;
Lead thou me on,
Keep thou my feet; I do not ask to see
The distant scene; one step enough for me,
Lead thou me on."

FINIS.